Personality Disorders:
New Perspectives on
Diagnostic Validity

ROGRESS _IN_
SYCHIATRY
Series

David Spiegel, M.D.
Series Editor

Personality Disorders: New Perspectives on Diagnostic Validity

Edited by
John M. Oldham, M.D.

Washington, DC
London, England

Copyright © 1991 American Psychiatric Press, Inc.
ALL RIGHTS RESERVED
Manufactured in the United States of America
First Edition   93 92 91 90   4 3 2 1

American Psychiatric Press, Inc.
1400 K Street, N.W.
Washington, DC, 20005

The paper used in this publication meets the minimum requirements of the American National Standard for Information Sciences—Permanence of Paper for Printed Library Materials, ANSI Z39.48-1984.   ∞

Library of Congress Cataloging-in-Publication Data

Personality disorders: new perspectives on diagnostic validity/ edited by John M. Oldham.—1st ed.
    p.   cm. — (Progress in psychiatry)
    Includes bibliographical references.
    ISBN 0-88048-113-7 (alk. paper)
    1. Personality disorders—Diagnosis. I. Oldham, John M.
II. Series.
    [DNLM: 1. Personality Disorders—diagnosis. WM 190 P4673]
RC554.P485   1990
616.85′8—dc20

DNLM/DLC   89-18135
for Library of Congress   CIP

British Cataloguing in Publication Data

A CIP record is available from the British Library.

Contents

Contributors

Joseph Barrash, Ph.D.
Clinical Psychologist, Minneapolis, Minnesota

Donald W. Black, M.D.
Assistant Professor of Psychiatry, University of Iowa College of Medicine, Iowa City, Iowa

Jack Cornelius, M.D.
Assistant Professor of Psychiatry, University of Pittsburgh, Western Psychiatric Institute and Clinic, Pittsburgh, Pennsylvania

William H. Coryell, M.D.
Professor of Psychiatry, University of Iowa College of Medicine, Iowa City, Iowa

Wayne S. Fenton, M.D.
Adjunctive Clinical Professor of Psychiatry, George Washington University School of Medicine, Washington, D.C.

Allen J. Frances, M.D.
Professor of Psychiatry, Cornell University Medical College, New York, New York

Minna Fyer, M.D.
Research Psychiatrist, Department of Psychiatry, The New York Hospital, Cornell University Medical College, New York, New York

Anselm George, M.D.
Assistant Professor of Psychiatry, University of Pittsburgh, Western Psychiatric Institute and Clinic, Pittsburgh, Pennsylvania

John G. Gunderson, M.D.
Associate Professor of Psychiatry, Harvard Medical School; Director, Psychosocial Research Program, McLean Hospital, Belmont, Massachusetts

Monica Harris, Ph.D.
Assistant Professor of Psychology, University of Kentucky, Lexington, Kentucky

Steven Hyler, M.D.
Associate Clinical Professor of Psychiatry, Columbia University College of Physicians and Surgeons, New York, New York

Douglas N. Jackson, Ph.D.
Senior Professor of Psychology, University of Western Ontario, London, Ontario, Canada

Lawrence B. Jacobsberg, M.D.
Assistant Professor of Psychiatry, Cornell University Medical College, New York, New York

Richard J. Kavoussi, M.D.
Assistant Clinical Professor of Psychiatry, Columbia University College of Physicians and Surgeons, New York, New York

David Kellman, M.D.
Instructor in Clinical Psychiatry, Columbia University College of Physicians and Surgeons, New York, New York

W. John Livesley, M.B.Ch.B, Ph.D.
Professor of Psychiatry, University of British Columbia, Vancouver, British Columbia, Canada

Donna Manning, M.D.
Clinical Assistant Professor of Psychiatry, The New York Hospital, Cornell University Medical College, New York, New York

Thomas H. McGlashan, M.D.
Clinical Professor of Psychiatry, Uniformed Services University of the Health Sciences; Research Professor, Department of Psychiatry, University of Maryland School of Medicine, Baltimore; Director, Chestnut Lodge Research Institute, Rockville, Maryland

Swami Nathan, M.D.
Assistant Professor of Psychiatry, Vice Chairman, Department of Psychiatry, Medical College of Pennsylvania, Philadelphia, Pennsylvania

Russell Noyes, M.D.
Professor of Psychiatry, University of Iowa College of Medicine, Iowa City, Iowa

John M. Oldham, M.D.
Professor of Clinical Psychiatry, Associate Chairman, Department of Psychiatry, Columbia University College of Physicians and Surgeons, New York, New York

J. Christopher Perry, M.P.H, M.D.
Assistant Professor in Psychiatry, Harvard Medical School, Cambridge, Massachusetts

Bruce Pfohl, M.D.
Associate Professor of Psychiatry, University of Iowa College of Medicine, Iowa City, Iowa

Elsa Ronningstam, Ph.D.
Clinical and Research Fellow, Psychosocial Research Program, McLean Hospital, Belmont, Massachusetts

Lyle Rosnick, M.D.
Assistant Clinical Professor of Psychiatry, Columbia University College of Physicians and Surgeons, New York, New York

Patricia Schulz, M.S.W.
Social Worker, Cleveland Heights, Ohio

Larry J. Siever, M.D.
Professor of Psychiatry, Mt. Sinai School of Medicine, New York, New York

Andrew Skodol, M.D.
Associate Clinical Professor of Psychiatry, Columbia University College of Physicians and Surgeons, New York, New York

Paul H. Soloff, M.D.
Associate Professor of Psychiatry, University of Pittsburgh, Western Psychiatric Institute and Clinic, Pittsburgh, Pennsylvania

Thomas A. Widiger, Ph.D.
Professor of Psychology, University of Kentucky College of Arts and Sciences, Lexington, Kentucky

Introduction to the
Progress in Psychiatry Series

The *Progress in Psychiatry* Series is designed to capture in print the excitement that comes from assembling a diverse group of experts from various locations to examine in detail the newest information about a developing aspect of psychiatry. This series emerged as a collaboration between the American Psychiatric Association's (APA) Scientific Program Committee and the American Psychiatric Press, Inc. Great interest is generated by a number of the symposia presented each year at the APA Annual Meeting, and we realized that much of the information presented there, carefully assembled by people who are deeply immersed in a given area, would unfortunately not appear together in print. The symposia sessions at the Annual Meetings provide an unusual opportunity for experts who otherwise might not meet on the same platform to share their diverse viewpoints for a period of 3 hours. Some new themes are repeatedly reinforced and gain credence, while in other instances disagreements emerge, enabling the audience and now the reader to reach informed decisions about new directions in the field. The *Progress in Psychiatry* Series allows us to publish and capture some of the best of the symposia and thus provide an in-depth treatment of specific areas that might not otherwise be presented in broader review formats.

Psychiatry is by nature an interface discipline, combining the study of mind and brain, of individual and social environments, of the humane and the scientific. Therefore, progress in the field is rarely linear—it often comes from unexpected sources. Further, new developments emerge from an array of viewpoints that do not necessarily provide immediate agreement but rather expert examination of the issues. We intend to present innovative ideas and data that will enable you, the reader, to participate in this process.

We believe the *Progress in Psychiatry* Series will provide you with an opportunity to review timely new information in specific fields of interest as they are developing. We hope you find that the excitement of the presentations is captured in the written word and that this book proves to be informative and enjoyable reading.

David Spiegel, M.D.
Series Editor
Progress in Psychiatry Series

Progress in Psychiatry Series Titles

The Borderline: Current Empirical Research (#1)
Edited by Thomas H. McGlashan, M.D.

Premenstrual Syndrome: Current Findings and Future Directions (#2)
Edited by Howard J. Osofsky, M.D., Ph.D., and Susan J. Blumenthal, M.D.

Treatment of Affective Disorders in the Elderly (#3)
Edited by Charles A. Shamoian, M.D.

Post-Traumatic Stress Disorder in Children (#4)
Edited by Spencer Eth, M.D., and Robert S. Pynoos, M.D., M.P.H.

The Psychiatric Implications of Menstruation (#5)
Edited by Judith H. Gold, M.D., F.R.C.P. (C)

Can Schizophrenia Be Localized in the Brain? (#6)
Edited by Nancy C. Andreasen, M.D., Ph.D.

Medical Mimics of Psychiatric Disorders (#7)
Edited by Irl Extein, M.D., and Mark S. Gold, M.D.

Biopsychosocial Aspects of Bereavement (#8)
Edited by Sidney Zisook, M.D.

Psychiatric Pharmacosciences of Children and Adolescents (#9)
Edited by Charles Popper, M.D.

Psychobiology of Bulimia (#10)
Edited by James I. Hudson, M.D., and Harrison G. Pope, Jr., M.D.

Cerebral Hemisphere Function in Depression (#11)
Edited by Marcel Kinsbourne, M.D.

Eating Behavior in Eating Disorders (#12)
Edited by B. Timothy Walsh, M.D.

Tardive Dyskinesia: Biological Mechanisms and Clinical Aspects (#13)
Edited by Marion E. Wolf, M.D., and Aron D. Mosnaim, Ph.D.

Current Approaches to the Prediction of Violence (#14)
Edited by David A. Brizer, M.D., and Martha L. Crowner, M.D.

Treatment of Tricyclic-Resistant Depression (#15)
Edited by Irl L. Extein, M.D.

Depressive Disorders and Immunity (#16)
Edited by Andrew H. Miller, M.D.

Introduction

In an essay reviewing the question of the validity of the Diagnostic Interview Schedule in the Epidemiologic Catchment Area Project, Robins refers to both the problems and the challenge of assessing validity, and points out that psychiatry lacks laboratory tests that can definitively assess the presence or absence of a disorder (Robins 1985). In this article, Robins focused on the validity of a newly developed assessment instrument, i.e., whether a new structured interview validly assessed the presence or absence of the disorders it was designed to measure. In an earlier article, Robins and Guze reviewed the broader question of validity of diagnostic categories suggesting, in the absence of laboratory tests, that external correlates of illness such as positive family history, treatment response, and outcome on follow-up may be our best validators (Robins and Guze 1970).

Validity, as a category applied to psychiatric diagnosis and assessment, encompasses several meanings. Descriptive validity or construct validity refers to whether or not a particular diagnostic category is clinically meaningful. Does a diagnosis define a group of patients who generally share a form of psychopathology that is reasonably unique and different from other known forms of psychopathology? Does the diagnosis refer to an illness rather than another phenomenon, such as a cultural effect? Does it define a treatable condition? And so on — i.e., is the condition real, and is it sensible and meaningful to clinicians?

Once a diagnosis is agreed to be valid, then a valid method to assess the presence or absence of the disorder needs to be developed, especially for research purposes. Generally, there is no foolproof gold standard against which to measure the validity, or the absence of validity, of a particular diagnostic assessment method. The collective wisdom of experienced clinicians is most often accepted as the norm. Spitzer suggested a particular standard that involves input from an experienced clinician who uses multiple sources of data, including observations of the patient over time (Spitzer 1983). (See Chapter 3, this volume.) When an assessment instrument has been accepted as valid for use by the research community, then a new instrument can be compared with the existing one for diagnoses assessed by both instruments.

Personality disorders present many challenges in the areas of construct validity and assessment validity. DSM-III (American Psychiatric Association 1980), maintaining its traditional categorical diagnostic system for personality disorders, established a separate axis for these disorders and established for the first time sets of criteria by which, presumably in a reasonably objective (measurable or observable) way, to arrive at these diagnoses. Some DSM-III Axis II diagnoses were unchanged from earlier versions of the diagnostic manual, but some earlier terms were dropped, and several new diagnostic terms were added (Blashfield and McElroy 1989; Oldham 1989). Particularly for new diagnoses (e.g., borderline, narcissistic, avoidant, self-defeating), there continues to be controversy about their construct or descriptive validity. New methods of assessment for research purposes have been developed for DSM-III Axis II, but the assessment validity of these instruments is complicated by both concerns about the construct validity of the new diagnoses and the lack of any systematic and comprehensive previously existing methods to assess DSM-III and DSM-III-R (American Psychiatric Association 1987) personality disorders. Most widely used assessment instruments that were based on the Research Diagnostic Criteria (Spitzer et al. 1978) included only one or two personality disorders. As one of the developers of the Personality Disorder Examination (PDE) (Loranger et al. 1987), I recall many discussions about our task of developing an instrument to assess DSM-III Axis II disorders as defined by the diagnostic criteria, whether or not we agreed with the criteria. When presenting the PDE, which was sponsored by the National Institute of Mental Health, to the World Health Organization, many questions initially raised about the PDE turned out to be questions about the validity of the personality disorder diagnostic categories of DSM-III.

This volume addresses many of these questions about validity as applied to personality disorders, defined by DSM-III or DSM-III-R. Livesley and Jackson present in Chapter 1 an overview of the concept of construct validity, debating the categorical system adopted by DSM-III in contrast to a dimensional diagnostic system. Perry, in Chapter 2, reviews the arguments for and against the use of longitudinal data to validate the personality disorder diagnoses. In Chapter 3, Skodol et al. present a methodology along with pilot data implementing the standard proposed by Spitzer. The use of biologic markers as validators of personality diagnoses is described in Chapter 4 by Kavoussi and Siever, followed by the focus by Soloff et al. in Chapter 5 on borderline subtypes using response to psychopharmacological intervention as their method to approach validity. The construct validity of a new category, narcissistic personality disorder, is examined by Gunderson and Ronningstam in Chapter 6, in which they present a newly developed instrument, the Diagnostic Interview for Narcissistic Personality Disorder. With the Chestnut Lodge data, McGlashan and Fenton (Chapter 7) study the validity of the decision by DSM-III to establish two separate diagnostic categories, borderline and schizotypal; they evaluate the diagnostic efficiency of the specific criteria for the two disorders, attempting to ascertain prototypic descriptions of each. Finally, the last two chapters look at the question of comorbidity. Pfohl et al. in Chapter 8 look at selected aspects of Axis I and Axis II comorbidity, with particular attention to the co-occurrence of depression and Axis II diagnoses. In Chapter 9, Widiger et al. examine patterns of comorbidity among Axis II disorders, reviewing the strengths and weaknesses of the various statistical methods of analyzing these data.

The questions inherent in the concepts of descriptive and assessment validity are complex and inevitably inconclusive. The collection of chapters in this volume, some of them initially presented at a symposium at an annual meeting of the American Psychiatric Association, however, constitute a sophisticated cross section of the critical aspects of these questions as they apply to personality disorders.

REFERENCES

American Psychiatric Association: Diagnostic and Statistical Manual of Mental Disorders, 3rd Edition. Washington, DC, American Psychiatric Association, 1980

American Psychiatric Association: Diagnostic and Statistical Manual of Mental Disorders, 3rd Edition, Revised. Washington, DC, American Psychiatric Association, 1987

Blashfield RK, McElroy RA: Ontology of personality disorder categories. Psychiatric Annals 19:126–131, 1989

Loranger AW, Susman V, Oldham J, et al: The Personality Disorder Examination: a preliminary report. J Pers Disord 1:1–13, 1987

Oldham JM: Diagnosis of the neuroses, in Modern Perspectives in the Psychiatry of the Neuroses. Edited by Howells JG. New York, Brunner/Mazel, 1989

Robins E, Guze S: Establishment of diagnostic validity in psychiatric illness: its application to schizophrenia. Am J Psychiatry 126:983–987, 1970

Robins LN: Epidemiology: reflections on testing the validity of psychiatric interviews. Arch Gen Psychiatry 42:918–924, 1985

Spitzer RL: Psychiatric diagnosis: are clinicians still necessary? Compr Psychiatry 24:399–411, 1983

Spitzer RL, Endicott J, Robins E: Research diagnostic criteria: rationale and reliability. Arch Gen Psychiatry 35:773–789, 1978

Chapter 1

Construct Validity and Classification of Personality Disorders

W. John Livesley, M.B.Ch.B., Ph.D.
Douglas N. Jackson, Ph.D.

Chapter 1

Construct Validity and Classification of Personality Disorders

The scientific evaluation of a classification system requires several steps, each necessary, but none in itself sufficient for establishing validity. Although various criteria have been proposed for evaluating psychiatric classifications (Blashfield and Draguns 1976a, 1976b) and for establishing the validity of specific diagnoses (Feighner et al. 1972), the construct validation framework (Loevinger 1957) provides the most integrated approach to the problem (Skinner 1981, 1986). As conceptualized by Loevinger, construct validity has three aspects: substantive, structural, and external components. Major features of the substantive component are definitional and involve developing precise definitions of diagnoses and their components based on theoretical rather than empirical considerations. Diagnostic items or exemplars are then selected for conformity to the definition. Definitions of diagnoses and diagnostic exemplars form a theoretically derived classification that is subsequently evaluated empirically. The structural component refers to the extent to which the relationship between components of the classification are supported by empirical evidence. With the classification of personality disorders this involves demonstrating empirically that diagnostic criteria are organized into the diagnoses postulated by theoretical classification. The external component of validity is established by showing that the classification predicts clinical outcomes, has descriptive validity, and is generalizable across different populations.

In this chapter we will outline the application of construct validation principles to the development of a classification of personality

The preparation of this chapter was supported in part by a National Health Research Scholar Award and a Medical Research Council of Canada grant (MA-9424) to W.J.L.

disorders under four headings: the importance of definition, the aggregation of diagnostic items, structural relationships among components of classification, and convergent and discriminant validity. In discussing these topics it will become clear that the steps required to establish a valid classification are iterative in the sense that findings from one phase may be used to modify previous phases. The theoretical classification is continually reformulated on the basis of empirical observations so that it successively approximates a valid system.

Although considerable progress has been made in recent years, it is apparent that current classifications of personality disorders, such as the versions of DSM-III (American Psychiatric Association 1980), are far from satisfactory. Criticisms directed at these systems include their arbitrariness in terms of both the variety and nature of the disorders listed, and their defining criteria. Other concerns are poor interobserver agreement (Mellsop et al. 1982), low internal consistency of diagnostic concepts (Morey 1988a, 1988b; Pfohl et al. 1986), and limited evidence for the validity of many diagnoses (Frances and Widiger 1986). Although attempts have been made in DSM-III-R (American Psychiatric Association 1987) to present criteria in more operational terms by specifying specific clinical features necessary for a particular diagnosis, these features suffer from the absence of an accompanying rationale for their inclusion, the lack of distinctiveness among features relevant to different disorders, and criteria sets that include an unfortunate mixing of specific behaviors such as truancy (antisocial personality disorder) and more global stylistic behaviors and traits such as rapidly shifting and shallow expression of emotions (histrionic personality disorder) or interpersonally exploitative (narcissistic personality disorder).

Part of the problem with current classifications is that they have evolved in an informal manner. Most of the effort has been directed toward the contents of classifications, i.e., the diagnoses to be included and the criteria for diagnosing them. Little attention has been paid to the more formal aspects of the system, i.e., the principles used to organize diagnoses; the definition of diagnoses and their components; the rules governing the selection and evaluation of diagnostic criteria; and the evidence required to evaluate, revise, and validate the system. The failure to address these issues directly has resulted in a situation in which many of the assumptions underlying the system remain implicit. These assumptions should be stated explicitly because only then can they be applied consistently and subjected to systematic empirical test. When revisions to current classifications are considered, the objective should be a classification that can be stated as a formal model with an explicit structure that can be modified on the basis of empirical evaluation to yield a reliable and valid system. For these reasons, it is important to examine the scientific and conceptual foundations for the classification of personality disorders, one that will permit confirmation or disconfirmation of the basis for the diagnostic entities and their defining features.

IMPORTANCE OF DEFINITION

The first step in construct validation is identification and description of each diagnosis, including the behaviors and underlying constructs defining each diagnosis. This step is similar to the first of five phases that Feighner et al. (1972) considered necessary to validate specific diagnoses; that of clinical description. Definitions have a pivotal role in concept formation in empirical science (Hempel 1952). In fact, a central activity of science is the elaboration of definitions of concepts. The concept of temperature arose from primitive sensory impressions, but in modern physical science its extended definition encompasses many properties and ramifications, including molecular theory and the physical properties of many types of materials. A concept that made intuitive sense has become progressively more precise and elaborate as a result of theoretical and empirical progress.

DSM-III diagnostic categories had their origins in the need for health care professionals and others to communicate about patients (Spitzer et al. 1977). These categories were developed through a process of discussion and consensual agreement by expert clinicians (Skinner 1986), but the cognitive processes leading to the basis for the categories have remained implicit rather than explicit. In addition to serving as a form of shorthand to communicate about patients, the hope and expectation are that patients sharing a particular DSM-III personality disorder diagnosis will demonstrate similar behaviors in various situations and will manifest personality pathology that is different from persons with other personality diagnoses. But DSM-III diagnostic categories are accompanied by limited information about the general types of behavior to be expected of persons sharing a particular diagnosis. Most of the effort has been directed at listing diagnostic criteria and rules for combining criteria without a clear rationale for including or excluding specific items. Such a rationale would be provided by theoretical definitions of each diagnosis.

The failure to define the basic components of personality pathology contrasts with developments in other areas of psychiatric nosology where considerable attention has been devoted to defining basic phenomenology with a corresponding increase in diagnostic precision. Progress in developing a more satisfactory classification of personality disorders is unlikely until rigorous concepts are used to specify the components of each diagnosis and to define explicitly what is being classified. To achieve this, an explicit format is required to organize definitions.

Examination of DSM-III reveals an implicit structure in personality disorder diagnoses. The diagnostic criteria listed differ in degree of generalization. Some criteria are traits, such as hypervigilance or low self-esteem. Other criteria are more specific behaviors, such as serious absenteeism from work. Trait psychologists such as Eysenck (1951) and Allport (1963) have used a similar hierarchy of constructs to describe the organization of personality. The different levels in the hierarchy are superordinate traits or typal constructs, traits, generalized habits, and specific behavioral items. A similar structure could be used to organize descriptions of personality diagnoses. With this approach, personality diagnoses would be conceptualized as typal constructs formed from several traits. Thus, narcissistic personality disorder consists of grandiosity, need for admiration, entitlement, and exploitation. The diagnostic items are specific behaviors selected to assess each trait. Within this framework the trait is the main unit of definition and description.

DSM-III-R apparently adopts a simpler model—each diagnosis is defined by a number of behavioral criteria as if diagnoses were unidimensional. This is probably the result of a desire to develop behavioral criteria to improve reliability, rather than the assumption that personality disorders are single trait entities. The specific behaviors, although not explicitly defined as such, are presumably included as exemplars of a domain of behaviors relevant to understanding traits. Presumably, these traits in turn serve to define disorders. Thus, having two or fewer friends might relate to an underlying trait of social withdrawal or low affiliation. But because the link is probabilistic, and in DSM-III-R unstated, there remains some doubt about which behaviors are the best exemplars of specific traits, and which traits the diagnostic items are meant to diagnose. For example, having two or fewer friends might be equally indicative of the traits shyness or defective social skills. Therefore, the task of definition is to specify explicitly the traits composing each diagnosis and to define each trait at theoretical and behavioral/operational levels. Theoretical definitions would provide a precise statement of the nature of each trait and, whenever necessary, would also specify the way the trait can be distinguished from related traits. This process begins to establish the convergent and discriminant properties of the classification. Thus, important aspects of validity are built into the system at the outset rather than established once reliability has been achieved.

An Approach to Definition

The definition of personality disorders can be approached in several ways. First, diagnoses could be defined empirically using multivariate statistical procedures to examine the way the features of personality pathology cluster in a sample of patients. One problem with this approach lies in selecting the characteristics to evaluate. Personality diagnoses are manifested through an almost infinite variety of cognitive, affective, and behavioral characteristics so that any empirical study could only sample a comparatively small number. This creates a potential for bias in the initial selection. For this reason it is not possible to construct classifications that are devoid of theory. Theory is required to guide the initial selection of features and to construct initial definitions of diagnoses. A second possibility is to derive definitions systematically from personality theory. Various theoretical perspectives have been proposed for this purpose, including psychoanalytic concepts, factor theories, social cognitive learning theory, and structural models of interpersonal behavior (Frances 1982; Kiesler 1986; McLemore and Benjamin 1979; Millon 1981; Widiger and Frances 1985). Unfortunately, there is little consensus on the basic dimensions of personality that could be used as a basis for classification. This has led to the proposal that definitions be derived rationally from general clinical knowledge and theory (Livesley 1986, 1987a, 1987b). Clinical observation has resulted in a considerable body of knowledge about personality disorders. Much of this knowledge is implicitly applied in clinical practice and the remainder is found in an unstructured form in the clinical literature. The task is to organize this information into a set of definitions that are theoretical in the sense that they are grounded in general clinical concepts.

This approach has been used in previous editions of the *Diagnostic and Statistical Manual of Mental Disorders,* which were based on the clinical judgment of expert committees and editors. This sort of expert judgment is important, indeed essential in the early formulation of a diagnostic system, but two demurrers are in order. The first is that expert judgment should be gathered systematically and the second is that other kinds of evidence, such as that derived from empirical studies, should contribute to the classification. There are several advantages to the use of systematic over informal methods for compiling expert clinical judgments: 1) aggregated judgments of many clinicians are more reliable than informal consensual data; 2) the process of definition is less susceptible to idiosyncratic and political influences; 3) quantitative estimates of the prototypicality of descriptive features are available; 4) quantitative indices of the degree of independence and confusability of related personality disorder diagnoses can be computed; and 5) systematic judgments may suggest ways in which the number and nature of diagnostic categories may be revised, something that is not apparent when a qualitative consensus is achieved by a committee. Of course, expert judgments are not the only reasonable basis on which to build a diagnostic system. The construct validation process that we are discussing is relevant regardless of the way in which the classification is initially delineated.

An example of the systematic as opposed to the informal development of prototypical descriptions of personality disorders is contained in the work of Livesley (1986, 1987a). Recognizing that category boundaries are sometimes indistinct and that some traits and behaviors are more prototypical of a disorder than are others, the author assembled separate sets of trait and behavioral features for each diagnosis from various sources, including literature review, content analyses of clinical interviews, and expert judgment. Both trait and behavioral features were considered because the latter permit the compilation of multiple criteria for a particular trait. These items were used to construct questionnaires that were mailed to 2,960 North American psychiatrists, with each psychiatrist receiving a set of either trait or behavioral features relevant to a single disorder. Clinicians judged the prototypicality of each feature to a particular syndrome. Several findings emerged. First, judges showed high agreement: reliabilities ranged from .81 to .96 for traits and from .88 to .94 for behaviors. This conceptual agreement lent support to the prototypical approach to classification. Second, many features reported in the literature as descriptive of certain disorders were judged to be of low prototypical value. Third, despite general support for DSM-III, there was considerable overlap between the highly prototypical features of putatively distinct diagnoses.

The lists of highly prototypical features for each diagnosis contained some redundancy because most lists contained features that described the same behavioral dimension. For example, the highly prototypical features of paranoid personality disorder included "expects trickery or harm," "mistrustful of the intentions of others," "searches for special meanings," and "readily perceives hidden motives." All appear to describe behavior that might be labeled suspiciousness. Therefore, the next step in the process of definition was to reduce the list of highly prototypical features for each diagnosis into a smaller number of mutually exclusive categories by grouping together items that referred to a common behavioral dimension. In the case of paranoid personality disorder, the resulting prototype consisted of the following dimensions: vindictiveness, suspiciousness, hypersensitivity to negative evaluation, reluctant self-disclosure, blame avoidance, externalization, rigid cognitive style, anger at conditional positive regard, resentfulness toward authority figures, and fear of interpersonal hurt. Each dimension was then systematically defined. Definitions were based on the prototypical features from which the dimension was derived. Each step in this process of definition used procedures that were specified and hence the process was open to public examination in ways that are essential to the development of a scientific classification. The approach contrasts with that used in DSM-III where it is not possible to see how the final system was constructed because substantial parts of the process involved implicit assumptions and intuitive judgments.

Selection of Diagnostic Items

The traits defining personality diagnoses such as suspiciousness or low self-esteem are not observable and have to be inferred from observable behaviors. Thus, the next step in construct validation is to select diagnostic items that will provide reliable estimates of these latent variables. This involves explicating personality traits in terms of behavioral items because inferences made about the presence of concrete behaviors will be more reliable than will inferences about the presence of traits (Livesley 1985b). Behavioral items used to assess each trait should be selected initially for conformity to the definition of the trait. This helps to establish substantive validity of the classification. It is also important to identify behaviors that are highly prototypical of the traits that define the different disorders. Again, systematic expert judgments may assist in establishing preliminary sets of items. Therefore, a two-stage process of definition is proposed: first, identify the traits relevant to each disorder and second, identify behaviors prototypical of persons for whom these trait constructs are characteristic. The result of such a process is a theoretical taxonomy organized in terms of prototypes (Cantor et al. 1980; Livesley 1985a) or ideal types (Hempel 1965; Jaspers 1963; Wood 1969).

In asserting that criteria should be selected by use of theoretically defined traits, we are seeking to establish a scientific classification that can be modified and developed by use of empirical evidence. The argument could be advanced that this is already possible with DSM-III and DSM-III-R. The criteria proposed by these systems can be studied to determine their reliability, specificity, and sensitivity and modified in light of the conclusions reached. The problem with this approach lies in the length and unsatisfactory nature of the process. When criteria, selected arbitrarily without reference to formal definition, are found to be unsatisfactory the only recourse is to select new criteria. When substantive factors are used to select criteria and explicit structural relationships are postulated between criteria and constructs and among constructs themselves, the process of criteria selection and evaluation becomes systematic and orderly.

AGGREGATION OF DIAGNOSTIC ITEMS

Regarding the appraisal of the validity of diagnostic decisions there are at least two schools of thought. The tradition carried over from DSM-II to DSM-III was that diagnostic classification is based on the clinical judgment and experience of a committee of expert clinicians. The system of classification within this tradition can be viewed as the development of diagnostic criteria that are signs of the disorder in the sense that they are necessary and sufficient for a diagnosis. Thus, if DSM-III criteria are considered to be definitions of disorders, then diagnosis by DSM-III is essentially infallible (Widiger et al. 1984). The only error in diagnosis under such an assumption is that attributable to a clinician's failure to identify criteria correctly. The only sensible validity study under this assumption is one evaluating the reliability of different clinicians in arriving at a particular diagnosis. Indeed, most studies designed to evaluate DSM-III Axis II have been of this variety.

Another school of thought about psychiatric diagnosis is that DSM-III Axis II criteria are samples of the sets of behaviors that define the diagnosis. This represents a different approach to conceptualizing and diagnosing personality disorders to that adopted by the editions of DSM-III. If personality disorders are conceptualized as typal constructs or syndromes defined by a cluster of traits, then diagnostic criteria can be considered to be behavioral manifestations of these traits. Thus, the criterion of having two or fewer friends might be considered an exemplar of the trait low affiliation. As such, it can be regarded as one of a large set of behaviors that might have been chosen to assess this trait. For this reason we will refer to diagnostic items as *diagnostic* or *behavioral exemplars.*

Several implications follow from the notion of assessing samples of behavior related to an underlying trait: 1) diagnostic items (behavioral exemplars) should provide a representative sampling of the trait; 2) aggregating behavioral exemplars will provide more reliable quantitative estimates of personality traits than single exemplars; 3) the estimate of a trait should be reliable; 4) some criteria will be more prototypical (better exemplars) of a trait than others; and 5) the distinctiveness of related traits (i.e., hypersensitivity to criticism and need for approval) becomes an empirical matter dependent on the degree to which behavioral exemplars are uniquely associated with the targeted trait.

Representativeness of diagnostic exemplars. The traits composing personality diagnoses refer to classes of behavior and summarize general behavioral trends. If a trait is to be identified reliably, diagnostic exemplars must be selected systematically to sample all facets of the construct. For example, low affiliation (a feature of schizoid, schizotypal, and avoidant personality disorders) includes subclasses of behaviors such as avoidance of social situations, pursuing solitary interests, declining opportunities to socialize, and having few friends. Assessment of low affiliation should be based on behavioral exemplars selected to represent all these facets. Because traits refer to specific classes of behavior or specific domains of behavior, this approach is usually referred to as *domain sampling*.

Multiple exemplars. The reliability of the estimate of a trait increases with the number of exemplars assessed (Neill and Jackson 1970; Paunonen 1984). This fact has important implications for the formulation of diagnoses. Single behavioral exemplars are usually unreliable estimates because they provide only a limited sample of the behaviors included in a given construct and because the assessment of a single behavior is influenced by chance and situational factors. Moreover, the same behavior may arise from different traits or from multiple factors. Therefore, individual items are likely to show low sensitivity and specificity. Consequently, it is the degree and frequency with which specific behaviors occur rather than the type of behavior that have diagnostic significance.

The use of aggregated items to estimate constructs contrasts with the DSM-III-R approach which frequently uses single behaviors to estimate traits. To use our previous example, the presence of fewer than one or two close friends is used to assess low affiliation in schizoid and schizotypal personality disorders. However, even the most sociable people may find themselves with few friends due to circumstances so that this item alone is a fallible predictor of low affiliation. The use of numerous items to assess a trait reduces the error created by chance and situational factors. The chance components associated with a particular behavioral exemplar will usually not be present in other behavioral exemplars representing the same trait. When exemplars are aggregated, the valid components will accumulate whereas chance components will not.

Reproducibility. That diagnostic exemplars should provide reliable estimates of traits and diagnoses is self-evident. Studies of the reliability of DSM-III-R criteria, however, have thus far concentrated on agreement between observers and neglected other important aspects of reliability, especially agreement between assessments made with different sets of behavioral exemplars, and agreement between assessments made on different occasions and in different situations. Part of the evidence required to validate constructs comes from data demonstrating that different samples of behavioral exemplars generate the same diagnosis. This ensures that diagnostic exemplars provide unbiased samples of behaviors relevant to the trait or diagnosis. This requirement derives from the domain-sampling approach and hence DSM-III-R, which appears to be based on a different approach to selecting diagnostic items, has not addressed this issue.

Because personality disorders are conceptualized as constellations of enduring traits it is necessary to demonstrate that assessments are stable across time and situation. Again, little attention has been paid to this area using measures of DSM-III-R diagnoses. Studies using other classifications have shown that traits with an affective component are comparatively unstable compared with other types of traits (Mann et al. 1981; Tyrer et al. 1983). Studies of this type are required to identify the core features of personality pathology and to ensure that the classification is assessing trait rather than state factors (Frances 1980). If assessments are based on observations made by judges or raters, it is also necessary to show that assessments generalize across groups of judges to demonstrate that the ratings are not idiosyncratic.

Prototypicality. When a number of behavioral exemplars are used to provide an aggregated assessment of a trait such as suspiciousness, some items will inevitably be better exemplars of suspiciousness than others. For example, in our own studies, "questioning other peoples motives if they do something nice for one" was found to be more highly associated with the aggregated sum of all suspiciousness items than was "tests other peoples' loyalty," although both showed a statistically significant association. If the aim is to develop a reliable system for identifying suspiciousness or any other trait, then a systematic procedure is required to select the most prototypical exemplars. This is most effectively accomplished by selecting exemplars on the strength of their statistical association with other aggregated exemplars in the set. Thus, sets of exemplars selected initially for conformity to the definition of a trait can be supported by objective empirical data.

Distinctiveness of constructs and diagnoses. A consistent observation arising from the use of structured interviews to assess DSM-III Axis II diagnoses is that there is substantial comorbidity. More than half the cases meet criteria for two diagnoses (Loranger et al. 1987; Stangl et al. 1985), and 30% of cases meet criteria for three or more diagnoses (Loranger et al. 1987). One reason for this overlap is that the criteria for different diagnoses are often similar (Frances 1982; Livesley 1987a; Widiger et al. 1988). In some cases the similarity is obvious because the same criterion is applied to several diagnoses, e.g., no close friends or confidantes (schizoid and schizotypal personality disorders). Sometimes the wording of items varies slightly but otherwise appears to describe identical behavior, e.g., frantic efforts to avoid real or imagined abandonment (borderline personality disorder) and frequently preoccupied with fears of being abandoned (dependent personality disorder). In other cases overlap is less apparent because criteria are phenotypically different although they describe the same trait domain, e.g., constantly seeks or demands reassurance, approval, or praise (histrionic personality disorder) and easily hurt by criticism or disapproval (dependent personality disorder). The relationships between criteria and diagnoses are obscured in DSM-III-R by the failure to provide an explicit rationale for selecting criteria. The domain-sampling approach and selection of behavioral exemplars on the basis of their association with the total domain score makes the overlap between similar traits and diagnoses an empirical matter. The distinctiveness of related traits such as egocentrism and entitlement, or related diagnoses such as dependent and avoidant personality disorders, depends on the degree to which exemplars are uniquely associated with the targeted trait or diagnosis.

STRUCTURAL RELATIONSHIPS AMONG COMPONENTS OF CLASSIFICATION

The structural component of construct validity is evaluated in terms of the degree to which the a priori or theoretical classification is confirmed by empirical studies. The hierarchical structure of traits and behaviors that we have proposed to organize personality diagnoses and the issues associated with aggregation contain assumptions that require further explanation. These are the structural rules that govern the way components of personality descriptions should be combined to yield a diagnosis. The discussion of aggregation referred to two sets of structural relationships: rules specifying the relationship between diagnostic exemplars and the aggregated measure of the trait that they are intended to assess, and rules specifying the relationship between the traits composing each diagnosis. The assumption underlying the domain-sampling approach to the development of behavioral exemplars is that each trait is composed of a general factor to which each exemplar is related. Thus, the number of exemplars provides a quantitative estimate of the trait. This structural model not only determines how traits should be assessed, but also specifies procedures for selecting and evaluating diagnostic exemplars. Exemplars are required to correlate highly with other exemplars assessing the same trait but not with exemplars assessing other traits (Jackson 1971). Thus, internal consistency analyses and item analyses provide objective criteria with which to select and revise diagnostic items that contrast with the more subjective and impressionistic methods that have been used up to now.

The second set of structural rules that need to be explicitly stated are those specifying the association between the traits delineating a diagnosis and the manner in which trait assessments should be combined to give a diagnosis. Here the appropriate model is less clear and several possibilities may be considered. If a categorical model is retained, each trait could be judged to be either present or absent using fixed rules that specify cutoffs for each trait, and traits could be combined in a polythetic model as in DSM-III-R. With this approach it is not the amount of a trait an individual exhibits but rather whether a specified amount is exhibited; it is only then that a trait has diagnostic significance (Kendell 1975). If a dimensional model were used trait scores could be combined to yield a superordinate dimensional score. The advantages and disadvantages of these strategies need to be evaluated and an explicit decision should be made with regard to DSM-IV as to whether a categorical or dimensional model will be adopted. Given the current stage in the classification of personality disorders, different rules and models will probably be required for different purposes. Categorical models could be retained for clinical purposes because they are easier to communicate and apply. Quantitative research, however, requires a more detailed system of dimensions to provide specific estimates of constructs, at least until reliable and valid diagnostic entities have been established.

An important aspect of structural evaluation is investigation of the degree to which diagnostic features are organized into the diagnostic entities proposed by the theoretical classification. Multivariate statistical techniques are the most commonly used procedures to evaluate this aspect of structural validity (Blashfield 1984; Skinner 1981, 1986). The methods of factor analysis and numerical taxonomy (Sneath and Sokal 1973) are appropriate for determining a natural organization of traits into the clusters or fuzzy sets that constitute diagnoses of personality disorder. Although, as Meehl (1986) concluded, application of this methodology is limited by the lack of a cluster algorithm that is generally accepted, such methods will serve not only the aim of validating the classification, but will also provide a more objective basis for revision by suggesting hypotheses regarding the reformulation of diagnoses and the diagnostic system.

Multivariate statistical procedures have been used to examine the relationship between diagnoses (Blashfield et al. 1985; Kass et al. 1985), but few studies have examined the extent to which the features of personality disorders are organized into the diagnostic entities postulated by DSM-III-R. Earlier studies (Presly and Walton 1973; Tyrer and Alexander 1979) examined the organization underlying sets of trait ratings, but unfortunately in neither case did the investigators make explicit the basis for selecting the traits that were assessed. In addition, Tyrer and Alexander studied few traits, therefore some diagnoses may not have been identified because relevant traits were not rated. Nevertheless, results of these studies converge in that both identified four factors or clusters that show substantial agreement. Presly and Walton used principal components analysis to identify four components: sociopathy, submissiveness, hysterical personality, and obsessional-schizoid personality. Tyrer and Alexander also reported four factors: sociopathy, passive-dependence, anankastic, and schizoid. Recent studies that have examined the clusters or factors underlying a more exhaustive set of variables, based on either DSM-III-R criteria (Morey 1988c) or on traits systematically developed to represent the domain of personality pathology (Livesley 1988; Livesley et al. 1989), have identified many more clusters or components. The systematic application of these procedures, including studies of the stability of factors or clusters across independent samples, is required to establish structural validity of the classification.

CONVERGENT AND DISCRIMINANT VALIDITY

Construct validity also rests on evidence regarding convergent and discriminant characteristics of the diagnostic system. Although the diagnosis of personality pathology traditionally derives from the diagnostic interview, other sources of evidence are necessary to establish the validity of diagnoses. Convergent validity derives from evidence that different measures result in the same classification and that individuals receive the same diagnosis when assessed with different procedures, e.g., a structured interview, rating scales, or a self-report measure. Discriminant validity derives from evidence that diagnoses can be distinguished from each other, and that the distinction holds when different assessment procedures are used. For example, the distinction between two diagnoses made on the basis of clinical interviews holds when other measures such as behavioral observations or self-report inventories are used.

The validity, and ultimately the utility, of a diagnostic system depends on the degree to which it contributes to accurate prediction and understanding of behavior in situations other than the one in which diagnostic information was obtained. Since the publication of DSM-III, a primary source of evidence presented in support of the system has been data on the degree to which independent clinicians using DSM-III criteria agreed in their diagnosis. Although such data are necessary, they are not sufficient; what is required is converging evidence from independent sources. There are two levels at which parts or the whole of a diagnostic system might be validated: the level of trait dimensions and the level of diagnoses or superordinate typal dimensions. Thus, if a set of individuals showed many behaviors relevant to the trait of egocentrism based on information gathered in a diagnostic interview, it would then be appropriate to determine the degree to which this inference was supported by data outside of the interview situation, e.g., in the judgments of informants who know the individual well, or other measures of egocentrism, such as self-report inventories or behavioral observations. Similarly, it is necessary to show that narcissistic personality disorder diagnosed on the basis of a clinical interview would also be diagnosed if other sources of information were used. But if a diagnostic system is being evaluated, it must be determined whether the trait of egocentrism can be differentiated reliably from other traits, such as entitlement, both by diagnostic interviewers and by other sources of information. It is also necessary to show that narcissistic personality disorder can be distinguished from histrionic personality disorder, and that this distinction holds when different assessment procedures are used.

The reason for this requirement is that measures of individual differences, including systematic clinical judgments, require a special form of validation, one that takes into account the various components that affect a given set of judgments or measures (Campbell and Fiske 1959). Every judgment or measure of a trait or diagnosis can be conceptualized as being determined not only by the entity being assessed but also by the method that is being used to make the assessment. Thus, clinical judgments of the comorbidity of traits or diagnoses may occur because of systematic sources of error in the interview process such as impression management by the patient, or some other factor common to all clinical interviews. There are similar systematic biases in projective testing (Schafer 1954) and in the assessment of psychopathology by questionnaire (Jackson and Messick 1967). Each measure of a trait or diagnosis is really a trait method (diagnosis method) composite. For this reason it is recommended that every trait (diagnosis) be measured by several different methods and that several traits (diagnoses) and methods of measurement be studied simultaneously to distinguish the influence of biases due to different methods of measurement on different traits (diagnoses).

Note that this requirement transcends the requirements of reliability. Reliability depends on demonstrating the convergence of measures with maximally similar methods, e.g., the demonstration that two clinicians arrive at the same diagnoses using the same structured interview. Rather, evidence of convergent and discriminant validity using maximally distinct methods should be sought (e.g., hyperactivity measured in the context of other traits using both a clinical interview and a monitoring device).

Sources of Evidence for Convergent and Discriminant Validity

There are three major sources of evidence for the convergent and discriminant validity of personality disorder diagnoses derived from the clinical interview: 1) systematic judgments by observers; 2) self-report measures; and 3) laboratory measures, including objective behavioral observations. Within each category there is a wide range of possibilities. For example, systematic judgments of patients may be based on interviews with the individual or obtained from family members, peers, and other personnel involved in their care. Moreover, the judgments may be based on structured interviews and rating scales. Whatever structured technique is used it should be designed to ensure that the behavior to be judged is observable; it should also include a sufficient number of instances to sample the domain adequately and yield reliable measures. These features have not always been taken into account in the design of instruments that are currently in common use.

Questionnaire measures of trait dimensions relevant to personality disorders have many advantages and potential shortcomings. Among the advantages are: 1) economy of administration and objectivity of scoring; 2) the theory and technology that has accompanied their widespread use; and 3) the fact that they lend themselves readily to sampling systematically behavioral exemplars relevant to a trait or diagnostic category. Among potential pitfalls are: 1) potential for eliciting response biases and consciously or unconsciously motivated systematic distortion; 2) their own need for evidence of convergent and discriminant validation; and 3) the expense and time required for their development. There is little doubt that questionnaire measures of personality disorder dimensions will continue to improve in tandem with our understanding of the nature of personality disorders and of the technique of personality assessment. They hold promise for providing a basis for evaluating assessments via the clinical interview.

Laboratory studies and objective behavioral observations have been used infrequently in the investigation of personality disorders. A wide variety of measures are possible, ranging from the unobtrusive elicitation and observation of behaviors relevant to a given disorder to laboratory studies of physiological arousal after some form of stimulation. Although sometimes expensive and not always conducive to the production of reliable measures, laboratory procedures have the promise of offering convincing evidence of convergent and discriminant validity because the method of measurement and content of the measure are usually different from those used in clinical interviews, systematic judgments, or questionnaires.

CONCLUSION

The steps that we have outlined provide a coherent framework for developing a classification of personality disorders. Construct validation is especially pertinent to the classification of these disorders because of the lack of external criteria that can serve as a gold standard against which our diagnostic concepts can be validated. Under these circumstances validity derives from integrating evidence from various sources (Cronbach and Meehl 1955). Although this problem is shared with other areas of psychiatric classification, it is particularly acute in the case of personality disorders. Under these circumstances the most reasonable way to proceed is to develop a theoretical classification that is formulated explicitly to facilitate the empirical evaluation. This permits the continual interplay between theory formation and empirical evaluation that is an important feature of construct validation. Through this interplay the classification is successively modified so that it increasingly approximates a valid system.

REFERENCES

Allport GW: Pattern and Growth in Personality. London, Holt, Rhinehart & Winston, 1963

American Psychiatric Association: Diagnostic and Statistical Manual of Mental Disorders, 3rd Edition. Washington, DC, American Psychiatric Association, 1980

American Psychiatric Association: Diagnostic and Statistical Manual of Mental Disorders, 3rd Edition, Revised. Washington, DC, American Psychiatric Association, 1987

Blashfield RK: The Classification of Psychopathology. New York, Plenum, 1984

Blashfield RK, Draguns JG: Evaluative criteria for psychiatric classification. J Abnorm Psychol 85:140–150, 1976a

Blashfield RK, Draguns JG: Toward a taxonomy of psychopathology. Br J Psychiatry 129:574–583, 1976b

Blashfield RK, Sprock J, Pinkston K, et al: Exemplar prototypes of personality disorder diagnoses. Compr Psychiatry 142:627–630, 1985

Campbell DT, Fiske DW: Convergent and discriminant validation by the multitrait-multimethod matrix. Psychol Bull 56:81–105, 1959

Cantor N, Smith EE, French R, et al: Psychiatric diagnosis as prototype categorization. J Abnorm Psychol 39:181–193, 1980

Cronbach LJ, Meehl PE: Construct validity in psychological tests. Psychol Bull 52:281–302, 1955

Eysenck HJ: The organization of personality. J Pers 20:101–117, 1951

Feighner JP, Robins E, Guze SB, et al: Diagnostic criteria for use in psychiatric research. Arch Gen Psychiatry 26:57–63, 1972

Frances AJ: The DSM-III personality disorders section: a commentary. Am J Psychiatry 137:1050–1054, 1980

Frances AJ: Categorical and dimensional systems of personality disorder. Compr Psychiatry 23:516–527, 1982

Frances AJ, Widiger T: The classification of personality disorders: an overview of problems and solutions, Psychiatry Update: American Psychiatric Association Annual Review, Vol 5. Edited by Frances AJ, Hales RE. Washington, DC, American Psychiatric Press, 1986

Hempel CG: Fundamentals of Concept Formation in Empirical Science. Chicago, IL, University of Chicago Press, 1952

Hempel CG: Aspects of Scientific Explanation. New York, Free Press, 1965

Jackson DN: The dynamics of structured personality tests. Psychol Rev 78:229–248, 1971

Jackson DN, Messick S: Response styles and the assessment of psychopathology, in Problems in Human Assessment. Edited by Jackson DN, Messick S. New York, McGraw-Hill, 1967

Jaspers K: General Psychopathology. Translated by Hoenig J, Hamilton MW. Chicago, IL, University of Chicago Press, 1963

Kass F, Skodol AE, Charles E, et al: Scaled ratings of DSM-III personality disorders. Am J Psychiatry 142:627–630, 1985

Kendell RE: The role of diagnosis in psychiatry. Oxford, UK, Blackwell, 1975

Kiesler DJ: The 1982 interpersonal circle: an analysis of DSM-III personality disorders, in Contemporary Directions in Psychopathology: Towards DSM-IV. Edited by Millon T, Klerman GL. New York, Guilford, 1986

Livesley WJ: The classification of personality disorder, I: the choice of category concept. Can J Psychiatry 30:353–358, 1985a

Livesley WJ: The classification of personality disorder, II: the problem of diagnostic criteria. Can J Psychiatry 30:359–362, 1985b

Livesley WJ: Trait and behavioral prototypes of personality disorders. Am J Psychiatry 143:728–732, 1986

Livesley WJ: A systematic approach to the delineation of personality disorder. Am J Psychiatry 144:772–777, 1987a

Livesley WJ: Theoretical and empirical issues in the selection of criteria to diagnose personality disorders. J Pers Disord 1:88–94, 1987b

Livesley WJ: The factorial structure of personality pathology. Paper presented at the First International Congress on the Disorders of Personality. Copenhagen, 1988

Livesley WJ, Jackson DN, Schroeder ML: A study of the factorial structure of personality pathology. Journal of Personality Disorders 3:292–306, 1989

Loevinger J: Objective tests as instruments of psychological theory. Psychol Rev 3:635–694, 1957

Loranger A, Susman V, Oldham J, et al: The personality disorder examination: a preliminary report. J Pers Disord 1:1–13, 1987

Mann A, Jenkins R, Cutting J, et al: The development and use of a standardized assessment of abnormal personality. Psychol Med 11:839–847, 1981

McLemore C, Benjamin LS: Whatever happened to interpersonal diagnosis: a psychosocial alternative to DSM-III. Am Psychol 34:17–34, 1979

Meehl P: Diagnostic taxonomy as open concepts, in Contemporary Directions in Psychopathology: Towards DSM-IV. Edited by Millon T, Klerman GL. New York, Guilford, 1986

Mellsop G, Varghese F, Joshua S, et al: The reliability of Axis II of DSM-III. Am J Psychiatry 139:1360–1361, 1982

Millon T: Disorders of personality: DSM-III Axis II. Toronto, Wiley, 1981

Morey LC: Personality disorders in DSM-III and DSM-III-R: convergence, coverage, and internal consistency. Am J Psychiatry 145:573–577, 1988a

Morey LC: A psychometric analysis of the DSM-III-R personality disorder criteria. J Pers Disord 2:109–124, 1988b

Morey LC: The categorical representation of personality disorders: a cluster analysis of DSM-III-R personality features. J Abnorm Psychol 97:314–321, 1988c

Neill JA, Jackson DN: An evaluation of item strategies in personality scale construction. Educ Psychol Measure 30:647–661, 1970

Paunonen JV: Optimizing the validity of personality assessments. J Res Pers 18:411–431, 1984

Pfohl B, Coryell W, Zimmerman M, et al: DSM-III personality disorders: diagnostic overlap and internal consistency of individual DSM-III criteria. Compr Psychiatry 27:21–34, 1986

Presly AJ, Walton HJ: Dimensions of abnormal personality. Br J Psychiatry 122:269–276, 1973

Schafer R: Psychoanalytic Interpretations in Rorschach Testing. New York, Grune & Stratton, 1954

Skinner HA: Toward the integration of classification theory and methods. J Abnorm Psychol 90:68–87, 1981

Skinner HA: Construct validity approach to psychiatric classification, in Contemporary Directions in Psychopathology: Towards DSM-IV. Edited by Millon T, Klerman GL. New York, Guilford, 1986

Sneath PHA, Sokal RR: Numerical Taxonomy. San Francisco, CA, Freeman, 1973

Spitzer RL, Sheehy M, Endicott J: DSM-III: guiding principles, in Psychiatric Diagnoses. Edited by Rakoff VM, Stancer HC, Kedward HB. New York, Brunner/Mazel, 1977

Stangl D, Pfohl B, Zimmerman M, et al: A structured interview for the DSM-III personality disorders: a preliminary report. Arch Gen Psychiatry 42:591–596, 1985

Tyrer P, Alexander J: Classification of personality disorder. Br J Psychiatry 135:163–167, 1979

Tyrer P, Strauss J, Cicchetti D: Temporal reliability of personality in psychiatric patients. Psychol Med 13:393–398, 1983

Widiger TA, Frances A: The DSM-III personality disorders: perspectives from psychology. Arch Gen Psychiatry 42:615–623, 1985

Widiger TA, Hurt SW, Frances A, et al: Diagnostic efficiency and DSM-III. Arch Gen Psychiatry 41:1005–1012, 1984

Widiger TA, Frances A, Spitzer RL, et al: The DSM-III-R personality disorders: an overview. Am J Psychiatry 145:786–795, 1988

Wood AL: Ideal and empirical typologies for research in deviance and control. Sociol Soc Res 53:227–241, 1969

Chapter 2

Use of Longitudinal Data to Validate Personality Disorders

J. Christopher Perry, M.P.H., M.D.

Chapter 2

Use of Longitudinal Data to Validate Personality Disorders

The advent of DSM-III (American Psychiatric Association 1980) has stimulated research on Axis II by separating it from Axis I and specifying explicit diagnostic criteria. However, DSM-III or DSM-III-R (American Psychiatric Association 1987) does not yet offer a validated taxonomy of personality disorders. The science is still young, and clinicians and researchers are exploring each disorder to see how useful it is for their purposes. This is a Darwinian process in which the likelihood that each personality disorder construct will survive depends on how many different facts cohere around the term. These facts can be grouped into domains. One influential neo-Kraepelinian perspective lists five domains: clinical and demographic features, delimitation from other disorders, family studies, laboratory studies, and follow-up studies (Feighner et al. 1972). An example from classification theory describes four domains for validating the classification system and its constituent disorders: reliability, coverage of the field of psychopathology, and descriptive and predictive validity (including treatment response) (Blashfield and Draguns 1976). Both perspectives emphasize the importance of longitudinal follow-up or course for validating disorders. This domain encompasses facets of greatest interest to the clinician, who must predict the course of a disorder with or without treatment for a given patient with a particular diagnosis.

This chapter reviews the use of longitudinal data relevant to the study of personality disorders. Broadly speaking, this covers what can be learned from using the longitudinal perspective, although validation of individual disorders and the taxonomy into which they fit is part of that goal. In turn, the chapter discusses some of the terms, substantive questions, methods of data gathering and analysis, and impediments to conducting longitudinal research on personality disorders.

DESIGN AND LONGITUDINAL PERSPECTIVE

In medicine, epidemiology has supplied the terminology and guidelines for the design and interpretation of studies of disordered populations (Hennekens et al. 1987). Some of these terms are described below.

Cross-sectional studies take their observations from one point in time, whereas longitudinal studies examine subjects over at least two points in time (Bailar et al. 1984). Cross-sectional designs are economical in time and effort and most studies of personality disorders have used this type of design. These include most studies of description (clinical features, prototypicality, discrimination from other types); family studies; and biochemical, physiological, and psychological laboratory studies. These studies are useful for generating hypotheses that can be tested further with other designs.

Among longitudinal studies, naturalistic observational designs attempt to delineate factors associated with the development of a disorder (e.g., etiology) or to determine the natural course of the disorder (e.g., remission, relapse, chronicity). This is a powerful epidemiological design, which in medicine has often helped uncover the mode of transmission of disease even before the etiological agent was identified (e.g., needle sharing among drug users and unprotected sexual contact in transmitting the human immunodeficiency virus).

Other longitudinal designs attempt to affect some outcome relevant to the disorder in question. Experimental designs can attempt to isolate a mechanism of pathogenesis, affect the expression of a disorder, prevent it, or treat it once it has developed. Most biochemical, neurophysiological, and psychological experimental studies attempt to isolate relevant mechanisms of pathogenesis or expression of disorders. Treatment trials begin with individuals who already have a disorder and then administer a specific therapeutic regimen to ameliorate or cure the disorder. By contrast, intervention studies begin with individuals at risk for a disorder who have not yet developed it and administer a specific regimen to prevent its development. These studies require previous knowledge of relevant etiological factors which, if modified, might prevent development of the disorder.

Most studies of personality disorders are observational, although there is increasing interest in experimental studies. Of the latter, treatment trials are the most well known, usually examining the response to pharmacological agents (Cowdry and Gardner 1988), although some have examined responses to specific psychotherapies (Woody et al. 1985). Currently, no intervention studies have been designed explicitly aimed at preventing the development of personality disorders, although treatment of certain childhood conditions thought to be associated with the later development of personality disorders might qualify (e.g., childhood attention-deficit disorder with hyperkinesis and adult antisocial personality disorder).

Longitudinal studies are further classified on the basis of the time perspective. Case-control studies compare those with a disorder to those without it, so that subjects differ on output variables (Bailar et al. 1984). Retrospective case-control studies look back in time for factors associated with the development of a disorder (input variables). Cohort studies begin with a group of individuals for whom an exposure factor is known to be present or absent and then look for the subsequent development of a particular disorder or outcome. Prospective cohort studies use a forward-looking time frame, because they begin before the disorder or outcome has occurred. Most studies of causal factors in the area of personality disorders have used retrospective case-control designs. On the other hand, studies of long-term outcome have used prospective cohort designs. Some examples are the study that established the link between childhood conduct disorder and adult antisocial personality disorder (Robins 1966), or outcome studies of borderline personality disorder (Barasch et al. 1985; McGlashan 1986; Paris et al. 1987; Pope et al. 1983; Stone et al. 1987).

AREAS OF INQUIRY FOR LONGITUDINAL STUDY

This section describes areas of inquiry that can yield information useful for validating and treating individual personality disorders. The topics are presented in order, looking backward to forward in time.

Childhood Precursors

Childhood temperament is often cited as an important precursor of adult personality disorders. A prospective study demonstrates a relationship between difficult temperaments in children and later development of personality disorder traits (Thomas and Chess 1977). Some specificity has been shown that solitariness, rigidity, and hypersensitivity among schizoid children is retained in adulthood along with the schizoid diagnosis (Wolff and Chick 1980). Impulsiveness is well documented as a childhood trait in conduct disorder which is retained in adult antisocial personality disorder (Robins 1966). Cloninger (1987) suggested that extremes of three different dimensions of temperament (harm-avoidance, reward-dependence, and novelty-seeking) underlie the development of eight basic types of adult personality disorders. This is an interesting heuristic model that may guide prospective studies of childhood temperament.

Recent studies have examined certain environmental precursors of personality disorders. A finding has emerged across different case-control studies that adult borderline personality disorder is associated with childhood histories of trauma, including sexual and physical abuse and witnessing serious domestic violence (Herman et al. 1989; Zanarini et al. 1989), and of early separation and loss experiences (Paris et al. 1988; Soloff and Millward 1983; Zanarini et al. 1989). Prospective studies will be required to demonstrate the attributable risk for developing borderline personality disorder due to trauma, early separation, and loss experiences and other potentially relevant factors.

Future prospective studies of children may combine measures of temperament, environmental stressors, protective factors, and their interactions with follow-up into adulthood. Unfortunately, large samples of children at risk would be required to link specific factors to the development of different types of adult personality disorder types. However, only studies like this can give a clear picture of how etiologically relevant such factors are.

Age of Onset

DSM-III-R states that personality disorders display manifestations by adolescence or earlier and usually continue throughout adult life. Determining the age of onset is difficult for most personality disorders because the adult manifestations may take a different form in childhood and adolescence, or because only precursors of the disorder may be present.

One exception to this is antisocial personality disorder. Robins (1966, 1978) documented the essential continuity between childhood conduct disorder and adult antisocial personality disorder through follow-up of cases from a child guidance clinic and matched control subjects. The adult and childhood manifestations antisociality have in common is the advantage that they are observable behaviors (impulsive, aggressive, violating others' rights) that are easy to identify. Robins found that antisocial behavior emerged in most boys by age 8 but not in girls until ages 12 to 14 (Robins 1966).

Clinical lore suggests that the age of onset for other personality disorders is gradual, although empirical documentation has yet to confirm this. Both schizoid and compulsive behaviors are thought to fit this pattern (Perry and Vaillant 1989). Some disorders appear to blossom over a short interval. These disorders may remain latent until triggering events cause them to emerge, i.e., the assumption of adult social roles, or loss of familial support. These events may be partly socioculturally determined. For instance, individuals with borderline personality disorder often first come to clinical attention after a transition out of the home in late adolescence (e.g., going to college, moving away). The latent manifestation of borderline personality disorder before the triggering event is not clear. Interestingly, cultures with extended family structures may postpone some triggering events indefinitely and the disorder might never fully develop. This might explain why certain personality disorders are infrequently reported in some cultures. For instance, clinicians from India, where Western-style nuclear family structures are uncommon, do report cases of borderline personality disorder, but they are rare compared with dissociative disorders and acute psychotic episodes.

Stability and Natural Course

The personality disorder concept entails that a valid disorder should be enduring not transient. Hence, any personality disorder should be reliably present at two different points in time, at least in the short term. The long term offers a different situation, because there is reason to expect that personality continues to develop or change in response to various maturational factors (Vaillant 1987). Thus, short-term stability is required for validity but long-term stability is left open as an empirical question. This has important implications for assessing personality disorders.

One current controversy is whether borderline personality disorder is a variant of affective disorder, an idea partly suggested by the high degree of comorbidity between borderline personality disorder and depression (Gunderson and Elliott 1985; Perry 1985). If the borderline personality disorder construct is not reducible to affective disorder, it must be stable whether measured during or outside of an affective episode. If during a depressive episode a patient is diagnosed positive for borderline personality disorder, and when the depressive episode has remitted the borderline personality disorder has also remitted, then the diagnostic method has produced a false-positive. If all borderline personality disorder cases followed this pattern, it would argue that borderline personality disorder is not a valid disorder in its own right, but is an epiphenomenon of depression. Currently, there is no evidence for this conclusion. The fact that such cases do occur, however, offers a challenge to develop diagnostic methods that measure borderline personality disorder features without great fluctuations due to changes in mood state.

Long-term follow-up studies of personality disorders are rare.

Recent interest has focused on follow-up studies of hospitalized borderline personality disorder patients. McGlashan (1983) found that on follow-up interview after an average of 15 years, 44% of DSM-III–diagnosed borderline personality disorder cases were still the same. Paris et al. (1987) found that only 25% of patients diagnosed by use of the Diagnostic Interview for Borderlines (DIB) still met DIB criteria for borderline personality disorder after approximately the same length of time. Although such data might suggest that borderline personality disorder naturally remits, it is complicated by other findings suggesting that borderline personality disorder subjects receive high levels of psychiatric treatment (Perry et al. 1987a). This highlights the need to assess factors that might facilitate change and assess whether change has occurred over follow-up. Single-interview follow-up studies have a disadvantage in this regard because such facilitating factors may not be present at the outset.

Discrimination of one personality disorder from another over time is important to validation. However, there are several confounding factors impinging on this. First, errors in assessment at intake (false-negatives and false-positives) are compounded by errors in assessment over the follow-up. Thus, even if two disorders were valid and discriminable according to a gold standard, when diagnoses are based on single interviews, some subjects are going to switch diagnoses or meet criteria for both at the follow-up assessment, reflecting error built into the assessment process. Second, we have no reason to believe that personality disorder types are mutually exclusive, therefore some overlap is to be expected. In fact, a taxonomy of highly discriminable disorders in which concurrent personality disorder types were rare would be highly suspect, because it would imply mutually exclusive causal factors. By contrast, if two disorders often but not always occur together, it suggests some common etiologic factors. This may be the case in the comorbidity between borderline personality disorder and affective disorders noted above or between antisocial personality disorder and alcoholism (Perry and Vaillant 1989).

One way around the problem of errors or unreliability in procedures to delineate the natural history of a disorder is to build redundancy into the diagnostic process. The simplest way is to make repeated assessments over time looking for the development of a trend toward improvement. However, noting at what point during the follow-up when a subject no longer meets the criteria for a given personality disorder still is limited by the validity of the instrument. An additional approach is to assess the features of a disorder with different types of data. This can include structured and semistructured interviews about symptoms and behaviors, how the subject coped with life events, and anecdotes about interpersonal interactions. The closer the data are to real life experiences, the greater the likelihood that the final assessment will be sensitive to real life personality functioning. Structured interviews that obtain yes-no answers from subjects about their personality features may have a disadvantage in this regard.

Natural History of Associated Conditions

One aspect of personality disorders that is receiving increasing attention is the association between Axis II and Axis I disorders, termed *comorbidity.* The presence of an Axis II disorder may affect the outcome of the Axis I disorder or other associated condition. For instance, personality disorders are associated with subsequent suicide rates that are substantially higher than in the healthy population (Black et al. 1985). Specific personality disorders may affect the course of specific Axis I disorders. For instance, in one study, both borderline personality disorder and antisocial personality disorder subjects reported high prevalences of major depressive episodes and substance abuse in their histories (Perry and Cooper 1985). However, over the follow-up only antisocial personality disorder predicted high levels of alcohol and other substance use, whereas borderline personality disorder predicted higher levels of affective symptoms, whereas concurrent antisocial personality disorder and borderline personality disorder predicted lower than expected levels of affective symptoms. This suggests that it is not having any Axis II disorder but having a specific Axis II disorder that predicts the course of the Axis I disorder. Therefore, the importance of the follow-up is that it has greater power to detect specific relationships between Axis II and Axis I disorders than is true for cross-sectional prevalence data.

Natural History of Treatments Received and Treatment Response

Analogous to Kraepelin's discrimination of manic depression from dementia praecox based on differing courses, Stern (1938) originally differentiated borderline patients from neurotic disorders based on a negative therapeutic reaction to psychoanalytic techniques standard at the time. Subsequent studies have consistently documented that Axis II disorders in general have poorer than expected treatment responses. For instance, the presence of an Axis II disorder is associated with poorer outcome among depressed patients (Pfohl et al. 1984). Similar conclusions abound from examining specific disorders. Antisocial personality disorder has a poor response to any psychotherapy except in the presence of concurrent depression (Woody et al. 1985). Borderline patients spend more time in outpatient and inpatient treatment than those with other disorders (Perry et al. 1987a) and, even in the hands of experts, often terminate treatment before optimal psychological health has been reached (Waldinger and Gunderson 1984). When schizoid-schizotypal features are present, borderline patients have a poorer prognosis with psychotherapeutic treatments (Stone 1983).

As such findings accumulate, it is important to search for specific features of a disorder that predict a treatment response. Analogous to the model of pharmacological dissection advocated by Klein and Davis (1969), longitudinal studies should begin to examine treatment response as a naturalistic experiment. Patients may get better with some treatments but not others. For instance, several studies found that neuroleptics ameliorated certain symptoms in borderline personality disorder, such as anxiety and paranoid symptoms, but not the core features of the disorder like unstable relationships (Goldberg et al. 1986; Soloff et al.1986). This approach should help distinguish primary versus secondary, or specific versus nonspecific features of a disorder, which will also have etiological implications.

Longitudinal data observing the outcomes of both naturalistic treatments and of controlled treatment trials should help elucidate etiological factors that may differ between disorders or between individuals with the same disorder. Some of these features will cut across several disorders. One example is that global functioning at the beginning of treatment can be expected to correlate with global functioning at the end of treatment, but it is not a factor limited to the etiology of any personality disorder.

VALIDATION STRATEGIES USING LONGITUDINAL DATA: MULTIPLE POINTS IN TIME

This section describes techniques of handling data gathered over multiple points in time. The author would like to acknowledge the contribution of Philip W. Lavori, who provided many of these ideas in discussions over the past 9 years. Each of the approaches below is helpful for handling certain types of questions about validity or characterizing the course of a disorder.

Multiple Diagnostic Assessments

Disagreements in diagnostic assessment come from variance due to subjects, occasions, raters, criteria, and instruments. This adds up to a problem of assessment reliability and validity, a considerable concern at this juncture in personality disorder research. If the criteria for a disorder are held constant, the other sources of error can still lead subject diagnoses to vary widely among research centers and over time within the same sample.

One solution is to use multiple sources of data in a two-stage procedure for ascertaining a given disorder (Dohrenwend and Shrout 1981). In the first stage, the subject receives two independent diagnostic assessments with two different instruments. Individuals rated positive on both instruments are considered true-positives, whereas those rated negative on both are considered true-negatives. The discrepant cases are then subjected to the second stage procedure in which a third assessment based on early follow-up data is compared against the first two assessments. The discrepant cases are handled by a majority rules procedure that determines the rates of false-positive and false-negative cases, thereby providing an estimate of the sensitivity and specificity of the instruments used in the first stage. This procedure has been used to test the Diagnostic Interview Schedule, which was determined to have high sensitivity but low specificity for making the diagnosis of antisocial personality disorder (Perry et al. 1987b).

Longitudinal Trends in State Changes

Some features of the course of personality disorders can be viewed as changes in discrete states. An example is whether the subject is employed or not. These states might occur haphazardly or they might have a stable probability of occurring. If the latter is true, then long-term trends can be estimated for the state. Markov analysis provides a statistical method of testing this.

In one example, the author examined follow-up data to determine whether borderline personality disorder subjects used higher levels of intensive psychiatric treatments than comparison subjects and whether this was likely to continue over subsequent follow-up (Perry et al. 1987a). Markov analyses on the first 2 years of follow-up data indicated that the probabilities of moving among three treatment states (no treatment, outpatient treatment only, intensive in-patient/daycare/emergency treatment) followed a stationary second-order process. This meant that knowledge of subjects' immediate past and current states of service use predicted service use in the next follow-up, and that the probabilities of making a transition among states did not vary with the point in time examined over the follow-up series. Furthermore, the transition probabilities generated from this model did not depend significantly on diagnosis. This indicated that although borderline personality disorder subjects began using high levels of psychiatric services, borderline personality disorder subjects and non-borderline-personality-disorder subjects followed a similar process of service use over time. The model was further tested over a subsequent 2-year follow-up period; its predictions of which patients would continue to use the highest level of services were confirmed.

Longitudinal Trends in Continuous Measures of Personality

Follow-up studies often gather repeated measurements of continuous scales. Examples are the Hamilton Rating Scale for Depression (HRS-D), or self-report measures like the Symptom Checklist 90 (SCL-90). However, because the intervals between follow-ups may vary, subjects miss some assessments, and subjects entering a study later will have fewer assessments than those entering earlier. Therefore, classic repeated-measure designs may not apply.

One solution to this situation uses simple linear regression models (Diem and Liukkonen 1988). Repeated assessments from each subject are regressed to describe the within-subject pattern of change over time. The independent variable is the length of time since intake into the study, and the dependent variable is the continuous scale of interest (e.g., HRS-D score). The sample size for each subject is the number of follow-up assessments. The output for each subject is a set of summary statistics that include the mean score over the follow-up, slope (or rate of change), and an estimate of the subject's score at intake (y-intercept). When subjects' summary statistics are combined for group analyses, the means and slopes of subjects can be weighted in proportion to the precision of their estimates (i.e., degrees of freedom). These group summary statistics can be used to compare diagnostic groups or subgroups. Other intake variables may then be used to predict the mean value or rate of change over the follow-up.

EFFECT OF AXIS II ON AXIS I DISORDERS

Although there has been increasing interest in Axis II and Axis I comorbidity, research has been limited to studies of prevalence or the frequency with which one disorder is found given the other. There is much more that can be learned about comorbidity when the effect of an Axis II disorder on the episodic characteristics of an Axis I disorder is considered. The characteristics of an Axis I disorder, such as major depression, are usually thought of in terms of age of onset, familial prevalence, and syndromal characteristics such as melancholic features or dexamethasone nonsuppression. However, the main effect of an Axis II disorder may be on the temporal features of the actual episodes. This includes whether a case first comes to clinical attention during an episode of major depression, how long the episode lasts (time to recovery), how long the remission lasts (time to relapse), the annualized rate of depression onset over a follow-up study interval, and the total proportion of the follow-up interval in which the subject was depressed (Perry 1988). Life-table or survival analyses are well suited to handle the potential statistically significant differences of time to recovery or time to relapse when examining depressive episodes in groups of subjects with different personality disorders.

Some preliminary evidence that the above approach is useful is the finding that borderline personality disorder and antisocial personality disorder were associated with high recurrence rates of major depressive episodes over follow-up in contrast to lower recurrence rates in an affective disorder comparison group, bipolar type II (Perry 1988). Preliminary examination of this cohort also suggests that borderline personality disorder and antisocial personality disorder samples further differentiate themselves on the characteristics of the duration of the episodes (borderline personality disorder has a longer median time to recovery) and the proportion of time in major depressive episodes over follow-up (borderline personality disorder spends a greater proportion of the follow-up depressed). As studies begin to delineate the effects of specific Axis II disorders on Axis I syndromes, it will be important to understand what pathology is responsible for these effects. The results should point toward treatments that will affect both the personality disorder and the comorbid Axis I syndrome.

IMPEDIMENTS TO CONDUCTING LONGITUDINAL RESEARCH

Although this chapter has emphasized the value of longitudinal research, there are serious impediments to conducting and completing these studies. Systematic planning is a sine qua non. In the best of cases this begins with stating previous hypotheses and designing follow-up measures to test them. However, even the best research cannot anticipate everything, such as the change in criteria for a diagnosis or the addition of a new potentially relevant diagnosis or area of inquiry that occurs after a study has already begun. Furthermore, the element of chance discovery early in the course of a study can add new questions to be addressed in subsequent follow-up. Perhaps the best studies do not entirely avoid being a fishing expedition to some extent, but by careful attention to selecting variables of interest and assessment instruments they ensure that the fishing takes place in rich waters.

Longitudinal studies are expensive. It is desirable to maintain a consistent staff, so that frequent changes in interviewers and raters do not introduce additional measurement error or alienate subjects. The author has found that a certain percentage of subjects can be expected to drop out when a consistent interviewer with whom they have established a relationship leaves a study. Having several staff involved with each subject may mitigate this to some extent if only one staff person leaves. Another source of expense is entailed in the use of follow-along rather than follow-up designs. Follow-along designs require serial assessment interviews at short intervals that minimize the loss of valuable data, such as when an Axis I episode began or was exacerbated, or how the subject coped with a particular life problem that occurred during the follow-up interval. Single-interview follow-up studies are less expensive but they cannot be expected to provide a detailed picture of day-to-day personality functioning and the temporal relationships among life events, subject coping, and recurrence of symptoms.

Maintaining contact with a subject sample can be difficult in long-term studies. Loss to follow-up can seriously compromise the validity of findings and their generalizability. This is obvious for some questions, such as determining the percentage of subjects with a diagnosis who committed suicide. Although subjects always have the right to drop out, keeping in periodic contact with subjects who have withdrawn from a study can at least provide data on vital statistics, although the rich detail provided by the follow-up interview procedures will not be available. Researchers should not be penalized for this, because it is a fact of life that some subjects will withdraw. Loss to follow-up when subjects move without giving forwarding addresses presents a similar problem. It is important to make every effort within ethical guidelines to find missing subjects. To prevent this, when subjects enter a study, asking them for the name and address of someone who will be likely to know where they live over the years, obtaining a social security number, and maintaining a caring positive relationship with subjects can mitigate against complete loss to follow-up.

The sources of funding have a great effect on the continuity of longitudinal research. The requirement of frequent review and funding renewal places the long-term aims of a study at risk for losing funds due to shorter term changes in funding priorities or popular ideas in a review group. In addition, there is no guarantee that the funding agency will have the same sufficiency of expertise available among their reviewers each time the long-term study is reviewed for continuation. In the Old Testament when Joseph interpreted Pharaoh's dream that there would be 7 fat years followed by 7 lean years, he was also foreshadowing the nightmare of conducting a

14-year follow-up study! This is true, despite the obvious conclusion that data increase in worth with the length of follow-up. These vicissitudes can be buffered by a solid commitment by the researcher, his or her organization, and by funding agencies to support longitudinal research as a long-term investment. Given this perspective, waiting years for a data base to be collected that adequately deals with an important question is like putting away fine wine to age. The delay in gratification is offset by its eventual increase in value. The long-term follow-up study based on 10 years of intensive follow-along can be expected to yield much more than the single-interview 2-year follow-up. Nevertheless, it requires a certain amount of faith to begin a long-term study.

REFERENCES

American Psychiatric Association: Diagnostic and Statistical Manual of Mental Disorders, 3rd Edition. Washington, DC, American Psychiatric Association, 1980

American Psychiatric Association: Diagnostic and Statistical Manual of Mental Disorders, 3rd Edition, Revised. Washington, DC, American Psychiatric Association, 1987

Bailar JC, Louis TA, Lavori PW, et al: A classification for biomedical research reports. N Engl J Med 311:1482–1487, 1984

Barasch A, Frances A, Hurt S, et al: Stability and distinctness of borderline personality disorder. Am J Psychiatry 142:1484–1486, 1985

Black DW, Warrack G, Winokur G: The Iowa record-linkage study, I: suicides and accidental deaths among psychiatric patients. Arch Gen Psychiatry 42:71–74, 1985

Blashfield RK, Draguns JG: Evaluative criteria for psychiatric classification. J Abnorm Psychol 85:140–150, 1976

Cloninger CR: A systematic method for clinical description and classification of personality variants. Arch Gen Psychiatry 44:573–588, 1987

Cowdry RW, Gardner DL: Pharmacotherapy of borderline personality disorder: alprazolam, carbamazepine, trifluoperazine, and tranylcypromine. Arch Gen Psychiatry 45:111–119, 1988

Diem JE, Liukkonen JR: A comparative study of three methods for analyzing longitudinal pulmonary function data. Stat Med 7:19–28, 1988

Dohrenwend BP, Shrout PE: Toward the development of a two-stage procedure for case identification and classification in psychiatric epidemiology, in Research in Community Mental Health, Vol 2. Edited by Simmons RG. Greenwich, CT, JAI Press, 1981, pp 295–323

Feighner JP, Robins E, Guze SB, et al: Diagnostic criteria for use in psychiatric research. Arch Gen Psychiatry 26:57–63, 1972

Goldberg SC, Schulz SC, Schulz PM, et al: Borderline and schizotypal personality disorders treated with low-dose thiothixene vs placebo. Arch Gen Psychiatry 43:680–686, 1986

Gunderson JG, Elliott GR: The interface between borderline personality disorder and affective disorder. Am J Psychiatry 142:277–288, 1985

Hennekens CH, Buring JE, Mayrent SL: Epidemiology in Medicine. Boston, MA, Little, Brown 1987

Herman JL, Perry JC, van der Kolk BA: Childhood trauma in borderline personality disorder. Am J Psychiatry 146:490–495, 1989

Klein DF, Davis J: Diagnosis and Treatment of Psychiatric Disorders. Baltimore, MD, Williams & Wilkins, 1969

McGlashan TH: The borderline syndrome, II: is it a variation of schizophrenia or affective disorder? Arch Gen Psychiatry 40:1319–1323, 1983

McGlashan TH: The Chestnut Lodge follow-up study, III: long-term follow-up of borderline personalities. Arch Gen Psychiatry 43:20–30, 1986

Paris J, Brown R, Nowlis D: Long-term follow-up of borderline patients in a general hospital. Compr Psychiatry 28:530–535, 1987

Paris J, Nowlis D, Brown R: Developmental factors in the outcome of borderline personality disorder. Compr Psychiatry 29:147–150, 1988

Perry JC: Depression in borderline personality disorder: lifetime prevalence at interview and longitudinal course of symptoms. Am J Psychiatry 142:15–21, 1985

Perry JC: A prospective study of life stress, defenses, psychotic symptoms, and depression in borderline and antisocial personality disorders and bipolar type II affective disorder. J Pers Disord 2:49–59, 1988

Perry JC, Cooper SH: Psychodynamics, symptoms, and outcome in borderline and antisocial personality disorders and bipolar type II affective disorder, in The Borderline: Current Empirical Research, Edited by McGlashan TH. Washington, DC, American Psychiatric Press, 1985, pp 19–41

Perry JC, Vaillant GE: Personality disorders, in Comprehensive Textbook of Psychiatry, 5th Edition. Edited by Kaplan HI, Sadock BJ. Baltimore, MD, Williams & Wilkins, 1989, pp 1352–1387

Perry JC, Lavori PW, Hoke L: A Markov model for predicting levels of psychiatric service use in borderline and antisocial personality disorders and bipolar type II affective disorder. J Psychiatr Res 21:215–232, 1987a

Perry JC, Lavori PW, Cooper SH, et al: The diagnostic interview schedule and DSM-III antisocial personality disorder. J Pers Disord 1:121–131, 1987b

Pfohl B, Stangl D, Zimmerman M: The implications of DSM-III personality disorders for patients with major depression. J Affective Disord 7:309–318, 1984

Pope HG, Jonas J, Hudson J, et al: The validity of DSM-III borderline personality disorder. Arch Gen Psychiatry 40:23–30, 1983

Robins LN: Deviant Children Grown Up. Baltimore, MD, Williams & Wilkins, 1966

Robins LN: Aetiological implications in studies of childhood histories relating to antisocial personality, in Psychopathic Behaviour: Approaches to Research. Edited by Hare RD, Schalling D. New York, John Wiley, 1978, pp 255–271

Soloff P, Millward J: Developmental histories of borderline patients. Compr Psychiatry 23:574–588, 1983

Soloff PH, George A, Nathan S, et al: Progress in pharmacotherapy of borderline disorders: a double-blind study of amitriptyline, haloperidol, and placebo. Arch Gen Psychiatry 43:691–697, 1986

Stern A: Psychoanalytic investigation in and therapy of the borderline group of neuroses. Psychoanal Q 7:467–489, 1938

Stone M: Psychotherapy with schizotypal borderline patients. J Am Acad Psychoanal 11:87–111, 1983

Stone MH, Jurt SW, Stone DK: The PI 500: long-term follow-up of borderline inpatients meeting DSM-III criteria, I: global outcome. J Pers Disord 1:291–298, 1987

Thomas A, Chess S: Temperament and Development. New York, Brunner/Mazel, 1977

Vaillant GE: A developmental view of old and new perspectives of personality disorders. J Pers Disord 1:146–156, 1987

Waldinger RJ, Gunderson JG: Completed psychotherapies with borderline patients. Am J Psychother 38:190–201, 1984

Wolff S, Chick J: Schizoid personality in childhood: a controlled follow-up study. Psychol Med 10:85–100, 1980

Woody GE, McLellan AT, Luborsky L, et al: Sociopathy and psychotherapy outcome. Arch Gen Psychiatry 42:1081–1086, 1985

Zanarini MC, Gunderson MC, Marino MF, et al: Childhood experiences of borderline patients. Compr Psychiatry 30:18–25, 1989

Chapter 3

Development of a Procedure for Validating Structured Assessments of Axis II

Andrew E. Skodol, M.D.
Lyle Rosnick, M.D.
David Kellman, M.D.
John M. Oldham, M.D.
Steven Hyler, M.D.

Chapter 3

Development of a Procedure for Validating Structured Assessments of Axis II

The inclusion of diagnostic criteria for personality disorders in DSM-III (American Psychiatric Association 1980) has had a dramatic effect on the level of interest in these disorders among researchers in psychiatry and psychology. An indication of the extent of this effect is the eightfold increase in the number of articles published on the subject of personality disorder in 1985 compared with 1975 recently documented by Blashfield and McElroy (1987).

The provision of a separate diagnostic axis (Axis II) for personality disorders in the DSM-III and DSM-III-R (American Psychiatric Association 1987) multiaxial systems facilitates their recognition and allows for examination of patterns of comorbidity between Axis I and Axis II disorders and the clinical significance of their co-occurrence (Hyler and Frances 1985). Initial research results indicate that personality disorders may frequently predispose to or complicate the clinical picture of various Axis I disorders, including mood (McGlashan 1983; Pilkonis and Frank 1988; Pope et al. 1983), anxiety (Grunhaus et al. 1985; Reich 1988; Van Valkenberg et al. 1984), eating (Hudson et al. 1983; Levin and Hyler 1986), and psychoactive substance use disorders (Khantzian and Treece 1985; Kosten et al. 1982; Schuckit 1985); may adversely affect the treatment outcome and ultimate clinical course of these disorders; and may be significant causes of psychiatric morbidity and reasons for treatment seeking in their own right (Skodol 1989).

AXIS II RELIABILITY

Diagnostic criteria were included for all disorders (except one) classified in DSM-III because such explicit guidelines to diagnosis had been shown to significantly improve psychiatric reliability in research studies with various pre-DSM-III criteria sets (Spitzer et al. 1975).

However, before DSM-III no specified criteria existed for personality disorders other than the criteria for antisocial personality disorder in the Feighner Criteria (Feighner et al. 1972) and Research Diagnostic Criteria (Spitzer et al. 1978) and a definition of schizotypal features in the Research Diagnostic Criteria. Reliability studies that used DSM-III criteria have shown that certain Axis I disorders not rigorously defined before achieved respectable reliability (Spitzer et al. 1979). However, the goal of improved reliability via specified criteria has been more elusive for personality disorders (Mellsop et al. 1982).

Diagnostic criteria make diagnoses more reliable by providing explicit rules for summarizing clinical data into a diagnosis (Skodol and Spitzer 1982), thereby reducing so-called criterion variance among clinicians, but they do not by themselves ensure reliable diagnosis. Another source of error variance in the diagnostic process stems from noncomparable data between clinicians on which diagnoses are based. Information variance has been reduced by investigators of Axis I disorders by the development of structured interviews (Hasin and Skodol 1989) such as the Present State Examination (Wing et al. 1967), the Schedule for Affective Disorders and Schizophrenia (Endicott and Spitzer 1978), and the Diagnostic Interview Schedule (Robins et al. 1981), which structure the data collection process so that interviewers will cover comparable areas of psychopathology in their examinations.

Therefore, the 1980s have seen the proliferation of many structured assessment instruments for diagnosing personality disorders (Widiger and Frances 1987). Some of these are self-report instruments based on DSM-III criteria (Hyler et al. 1988; Millon 1985; Morey et al. 1985), but the more elaborate and ambitious instruments are designed for use by mental health professionals (Loranger et al. 1987; Spitzer et al. 1987a; Stangl et al. 1985) or lay interviewers (Widiger et al. 1986) to guide a clinical examination. The structured interviews have undergone or are in the process of reliability testing, and the reliability of at least some personality disorders appears to benefit from structured assessment.

AXIS II VALIDITY

A reliable or reproducible diagnosis is not necessarily valid; validity means usefulness. A psychiatric diagnosis may be valid if it conveys something about the person who receives it that is clinically useful. It may indicate a particular treatment approach or the future course of a symptom or syndrome. A diagnostic instrument is valid if it measures what it is supposed to measure (Cronbach and Meehl 1955). Therefore, in the case of personality disorder assessment techniques, an appropriate question to ask in addition to whether a particular instrument can be used reliably is whether it gives a valid assessment of an individual's clinical status with respect to Axis II.

Validating a personality disorder diagnosis or an assessment procedure for diagnosing personality disorders is complicated by the fact that no clear validity standards exist against which to compare the diagnosis or the results of the procedure. The results of a particular imaging procedure or electrical recording in medicine can usually be compared with a definitive test or even direct observation of a disease process. Most mental disorders have eluded definition by definitive laboratory tests, and, therefore, have been validated by their relationship to predictable external correlates such as positive family history, treatment response, and outcome on follow-up (Robins and Guze 1970).

Searching for an Elusive Construct

Personality disorders lack a clear underlying construct that can be widely accepted on which to base predictions. This is partially related to the fact that the personality disorders that are currently defined are a conglomerate of conditions with varying ontologies, probable etiologies, and levels of severity. For example, as Blashfield and McElroy (1989) noted, the DSM-III-R cluster A disorders (paranoid, schizoid, and schizotypal) were derived from a historical tradition of attempting to identify subtle clinical forms of major psychotic disorders that might share a common genotype or represent early signs of an impending severe illness. Several disorders in clusters B and C (dependent, obsessive-compulsive, histrionic) were derived from psychoanalytic concepts of psychosexual development. Borderline personality originated as a level of organization of the self and its relationship to the other (object) that was believed to be midway between what might be found in a person with a psychosis versus a person with a neurosis. Antisocial personality disorder was defined to be consistent with the long-term maladjustment of delinquent children.

Debates have recurred over whether personality disorders are more psychosocially determined rather than biologically based, as might be the case for many Axis I disorders. Also, are personality disorders distinctive psychopathological states or exaggerations of normal personality style or attributes? Are diagnostic categories suitable for describing personality abnormalities or would ratings on certain dimensions of personality, such as introversion versus extroversion or dominance versus submission, be more accurate and clinically meaningful? Is personality truly invariant across time and situation or are a person's ways of reacting always, at least in part, determined by situational or contextual factors?

In early deliberations on DSM-IV, the Personality Disorders Work Group struggled with a general definition of personality to rationally decide whether schizotypal personality disorder should be classified with schizophrenia and related disorders or if dysthymia is a personality rather than a mood disorder. One definition offered by Gunderson (personal communication, November 1988) included the proposition that personality disorders are a collection of behaviors and traits that are resistant to or do not respond dramatically to changes in the environment or to treatment. Many members of other DSM-IV work groups disagreed with the notion that personality disorders would not prove responsive to pharmacologic intervention because they argued all human behaviors ultimately must have a biologic basis.

It is possible that current classified personality disorders are not equivalent disturbances or that there is some supraordinate organizing principle that will eventually be discovered that will reduce these conceptual disparities. Cloninger (1987) has proposed a tripartite definition of personality consisting of three dimensions (novelty seeking, harm avoidance, and reward dependence) he believes have a biologic basis and can alone or in combination account for the phenomena of most of the currently defined personality disorder types. Whether his conceptualization of personality is more clinically useful than current DSM-III-R categories remains to be determined.

A Definition of Personality Disorder

DSM-III-R defines the core concept of personality disorder as: a *personality disorder* is a pattern of "behaviors or traits that are characteristic of a person's recent and long-term functioning since early adulthood ... that causes either significant impairment in social or occupational functioning or subjective distress" (American Psychiatric Association 1987, p. 335). Individual personality disorder criteria define a particular pervasive pattern, e.g., instability of mood, interpersonal relationships, and self-image in the case of borderline personality disorder, that is present over time in various contexts. Thus, the concepts of pervasiveness, stability over time, and generalizability as opposed to situation specificity appear to be the core concepts of personality disorder, as defined by DSM-III-R. Any instrument that purports to measure DSM-III-R personality disorders should be identifying behaviors and traits that fulfill these core concepts. There are many potential pitfalls to the diagnosis of personality disorders so defined (Skodol 1989).

Pitfalls in Diagnosis of Personality Disorders

Personality traits, particularly if problematic, have traditionally been believed to be more ego-syntonic, and thus more difficult for a person to observe in him or herself, than the symptoms of Axis I disorders. Frequently, the complaints of others (spouses, bosses, friends) lead a person with a personality disorder into treatment, rather than the person's own distress over or awareness of a particular maladaptive personality style. Clinicians have traditionally weighed heavily their own observations of the patient in arriving at a personality diagnosis, distrusting the patient's self-description. Diagnostic instruments for Axis II are based on the premise that a direct question about a trait, no matter how onerous, can be asked and the patient's answer taken more or less at face value. For example, a patient may be asked whether he or she is more concerned with his or her own needs than the needs of others in assessing histrionic personality disorder or uses other people to get what he or she wants in assessing narcissistic personality disorder. A clinician may override a patient's self-report, but considerable faith is placed in direct inquiry. Some interviews allow for information from other sources to influence judgments, but how consistently this is done and what weight, relative to the patient's report and the clinician's observations, is given to outside information is not clear (Widiger and Frances 1987).

All structured interviews in use for personality disorder diagnosis are administered in a single session at a given point in time. Instructions are provided to the interviewer to attempt to assess the patient's personality style and functioning with a longitudinal perspective, and questions are sometimes worded to instruct the patient not to answer the question solely on the basis of the present. However, it is known that a person's current state of mind, particularly if depressed or anxious, can influence his or her reporting of past experiences. Thus, in conducting an evaluation of personality with a depressed patient, what may appear to be characteristics of dependent or self-defeating personality traits may in reality be manifestations of a mental state which may be an Axis I disorder, i.e., major depression or dysthymia.

When a patient responds positively to a question about interpersonal behavior, he or she may be using a close, good, or poor relationship as a frame of reference. This may lead the evaluator to conclude that a style of relating is characteristic of the person, when it is, in fact, situation specific. Interviewers conducting structured interviews of Axis II are usually instructed to elicit several examples of a behavior or to find out whether several people have perceived the person to behave in a certain way. How often and how consistently this is done is unknown.

HISTORY OF THE LEAD STANDARD

In struggling to identify a validity standard against which to compare various structured instruments for Axis II, we were drawn to the concept of the LEAD standard. Originally described by Spitzer (1983), the LEAD refers to a longitudinal expert evaluation that uses all data. LEAD was born out of a controversy over whether a diagnostic assessment based on a lay-interviewer-administered Diagnostic Interview Schedule or a clinician's interview was best in cases in which the two disagreed. Spitzer argued that in the absence of an infallible diagnosis, a gold standard to which the less perfect diagnoses could be compared, the best diagnosis he believed was one made on the basis of an assessment conducted by an expert on a given disorder who had the opportunity to observe the patient not just once but over a period of time, and who had access to all available information that might be informative, including records from other hospitals or treating clinicians, family members, friends, and treating staff. Such a complete picture would yield a "state of the art diagnosis," given current limitations in our knowledge of the underlying etiologies and pathogenic mechanisms for most mental disorders and the absence of definitive laboratory tests.

We found the LEAD compelling as a validity standard for the structured assessment of Axis II personality disorders with maladaptive behaviors and traits that were by definition characteristic of functioning over time, present in various contexts, and not limited to episodes of illness (Skodol et al. 1988). In the remainder of this chapter we will describe the development of a LEAD procedure on an inpatient service specializing in the treatment of severe personality disorders and our experiences using LEAD to validate structured interview-derived diagnoses of personality disorders.

A SETTING FOR STUDY OF PERSONALITY DISORDERS

The General Clinical Research Service is a 24-bed inpatient unit in the New York State Psychiatric Institute. It is a major teaching and research service of the Columbia University Department of Psychiatry. Over the years, it has been the site of numerous research protocols, including trials of psychotropic drugs and electroconvulsive therapy. But for the past 40 years it has served also as a long-term treatment facility for patients with severe character pathology. These patients have been the inspiration for the work of Hoch and Polatin, Kernberg, and Stone and although the names given the disorders from which they suffer have changed (i.e., from pseudoneurotic schizophrenic to borderline), the severe problems in functioning requiring treatment have remained the same.

Currently, approximately 15 beds are devoted to the study and treatment of personality disorders. Referrals come from a wide net of sources spread across the metropolitan New York area. Most patients have had many previous short-term hospitalizations and numerous outpatient therapists. Most previous treatments failed or were only marginally successful. Most referred patients are at or near the lowest points in their lives; they find themselves in a psychosocial crisis of such overwhelming proportions that only a major commitment to treatment and change holds promise for any future for them at all.

Patients are admitted to the service if a clinical team judges that they are highly motivated for change and able to derive benefit from psychodynamically based inpatient treatment. Patients must be deemed capable of tolerating limit setting and of profiting from insight-oriented psychotherapy. This judgment is based on an assessment of their assets (e.g., intelligence and talents) and their psychopathology. Patients must agree to have their family members screened and relatives must consent to participate in the program. Patients are asked to make a commitment to at least 6 months to 1 year of hospitalization.

The therapeutic approach is based on Kernberg's principles for patients with severe character pathology (Kernberg 1984). He recommends that a subgroup of such patients receive expressive psychotherapy in an environment structured to curtail acting out. The primary aim of psychotherapy is to enhance patients' awareness of their split-off and projected thoughts, feelings, and impulses so that they can develop integrated (i.e., more accurate) concepts of themselves and others. Treatment consists of three 45-minute individual psychotherapy sessions per week and participation in family, group, multifamily, occupational, and recreational therapy. Patients also attend a weekly patient/staff community meeting (Rosnick 1987). Medications are commonly used to treat Axis I syndromes of major depression, panic disorder, bulimia, or psychosis.

The clinical chief of the service for the past 12 years has been Lyle Rosnick, M.D., a psychoanalyst and general psychiatrist. Personality research is under the guidance of Andrew Skodol, M.D., Director of the Unit for Personality Studies of Psychiatric Institute.

Patients

Demographic characteristics of the patients admitted to the service for treatment over the past 2 years are: 66% of the patients are women; most are white and have never been married; average age is just over

27 years; and 90% graduated from high school, 75% attended some college, and over 33% have a college degree. Although over 75% had worked during the year preceding admission, less than 15% were employed at the time they were evaluated for admission.

Structured Assessment of Axis II

To begin a new program of research on DSM-III-R personality disorders, we instituted a systematic assessment protocol. All referrals were mailed a self-report instrument to assess personality disorders, the Personality Diagnostic Questionnaire, which was revised for DSM-III-R (Hyler et al. 1987). Referrals were instructed to bring this completed form on the evaluation day. The evaluation day consisted of three parts. First, potential patients met with a team of clinicians who interviewed them regarding their past and recent history and made a decision based on the principles outlined previously regarding whether or not each patient was suitable for and likely to profit from the intensive treatment.

After the clinical interview, each patient had two consecutive structured interviews administered by psychiatrists that focused on Axis II. We chose two interviews that contrasted in many respects: the Personality Disorder Examination (PDE) (Loranger et al. 1985) and the Structured Clinical Interview for DSM-III-R (SCID I and II) (Spitzer et al. 1987a, 1987b). Order of the two interviews was systematically balanced so that in one-half of the cases each interview was given first.

PDE. Questions in the PDE are grouped together by area of personality functioning. The six topical areas are work, self-concept, interpersonal relations, affects, reality testing, and impulse control. The interview is organized in this manner to provide for a smooth natural flow from one area of interest to another. Items are rated on a 3-point scale from absent, present but of uncertain or limited clinical significance, to present and clinically significant. Diagnoses generated by the PDE are made by a computer program that uses a series of algorithms, each requiring a score generated by one or more questions for a given criterion to be met. The number of positive criteria are added together and the diagnosis is made if the threshold number for a particular disorder (e.g., 5 of 9 or 4 of 7) according to DSM-III-R is met or exceeded. The clinician administering the PDE does not know if a particular diagnostic criterion has been fulfilled or a diagnosis given, because the number of questions per criterion vary as does the score required. There are too many complexities to memorize. Although the PDE includes questions to screen for major Axis I disorders, such as psychotic, mood, and anxiety disorders, there is no provision for a complete assessment of Axis I as part of the PDE. The clinician may have a notion of the Axis I status, but he or she is often uncertain.

SCID I and II. The SCID consists of two parts. SCID-I is a structured interview to evaluate a patient for the presence of 33 specific DSM-III-R Axis I disorders. On completion of SCID-I, the clinician has a clear idea of current and past Axis I disorders and their severity. The official version of SCID-II consists of a self-report questionnaire that the patient completes first, followed by a series of questions that are asked about any item scored positive by the patient on the self-report and any false negatives suspected by the clinician. The self-report questions are arranged randomly through the questionnaire, but the interviewer probes are organized by personality disorder. First, the clinician considers each of the criteria of avoidant personality disorder and then dependent, obsessive-compulsive, and so on through the 11 official DSM-III-R personality disorders and the unofficial self-defeating personality disorder described in DSM-III-R Appendix A. Each criterion is rated absent or false, subthreshold, or threshold or true. At the conclusion of the questions for a given personality disorder, the clinician adds up the number marked true and establishes whether the diagnosis is to be made or not made. Therefore, the clinician knows whether the patient is close to or far from meeting criteria for a diagnosis and which diagnoses have been made as he or she proceeds through the list. Such an arrangement of questions might have a halo effect, in that a clinician might be more likely to score a criterion near the end of a list positive if he or she thought that the patient had the disorder being assessed or negative if he or she believed the patient did not have it. Although a halo effect is usually considered to be an unwanted bias, Frances and Widiger (1987) have noted that it has not been demonstrated whether it is useful or detrimental to diagnosing personality disorders.

We used an older version of SCID-II in our research that does not use the self-report, but instead requires that all questions be asked of all patients. We were skeptical of the clinician's ability to suspect false negative answers to the self-report, and we believed that the effectiveness of a self-report screen should be empirically tested, rather than assumed effective, before the screen was incorporated into an otherwise clinician-administered interview (Hyler SE, Skodol AE, Kellman D, unpublished observations).

Use of contrasting approaches to diagnosis. We chose interviews with contrasting features for several reasons. First, because there is no clear evidence that one approach to the assessment of personality disorders is better than another, we decided to compare two approaches with the LEAD diagnosis as the standard. Second, because psychometric tradition (Campbell and Fiske 1959) teaches that the convergence of the results of tests or measures having contrasting features may yield more valid results, we wanted to study the convergence of these two interview approaches.

Table 3-1 summarizes features of the interviews.

DEVELOPMENT OF LEAD PROCEDURE

The LEAD procedure evolved through several stages. This section describes this process, culminating with our current version of the LEAD.

Personnel

Lyle Rosnick, unit chief, was chosen to lead the collection of data for the LEAD. His experience as chief of the service qualified him as an expert in the assessment of character pathology. Other senior staff members were chosen on the basis of their clinical experience and the unique perspectives they might offer on the patient's psychopathology.

An occupational and a recreational therapist participated in the LEAD. They observed patients in goal-directed activities in which they could monitor the patient's strengths and weaknesses with regard to ability to cooperate, to complete tasks, and to use leisure time. Social workers also took part. They contributed data from work with patients in group and family therapy. Finally, nurses were included. Nurses gave a perspective on daily ward life, including shifts not commonly observed by day staff, and a continuity of observation provided by daily reports and rounds.

Table 3-1. Comparison of features of Structured Clinical Interview for DSM-III-R Personality Disorders (SCID-II) and Personality Disorder Examination (PDE)

	Interview	
Feature	SCID-II	PDE
Interviewer	Clinician	Clinician
Organization	By disorder	By function
Scoring	By interviewer	By computer
Axis I assessment	Before	During
Axis I assessment	Complete	Screening only

Sources of Information

Information came from all conceivable sources. Psychiatric residents, social workers, and nurses conducted thorough clinical evaluations based on multiple interviews and reviews of records of previous hospitalizations and summaries and verbal reports from treating outside therapists. Primary therapists also had therapy sessions with patients 3 times per week and often met with family members. These observations were conveyed to Dr. Rosnick who directly supervised therapists. Dr. Rosnick also had the opportunity to observe patients and their interactions with others in a weekly community meeting where issues of community life were discussed. Each patient had at least one case conference in which he or she was interviewed in front of the staff by an attending psychiatrist who was not part of the ward team.

Interviews with parents, siblings, roommates, friends, spouses, and significant others served the function of providing informant information. For personality traits that are inherently difficult to observe in oneself or about which a patient might be uncertain how others saw him or her, informant data can be elucidating. Needless to say, perceptions of individual staff members also counted as informant data.

The critical feature of the information collected was that it was gathered over time. In the group of the first 36 patients who had the LEAD procedure, the average length of observation on the ward was 30 weeks. No patient was hospitalized for less than 6 weeks and some of the earlier cases had been inpatients for almost a year before the LEAD diagnosis was made.

A 6-month observation period allowed for several different phases of longitudinal study. All patients could be observed, when it was not detrimental to their overall condition, in a drug-free period of several weeks to a month or more. Many patients in this group had one or more Axis I disorders superimposed on their Axis II pathology that led to their eventual treatment with antidepressant, antianxiety, or antipsychotic medication as mentioned previously (Table 3-2). The longer the LEAD observation period, the more likely it was to be able to evaluate the patient in a state that was much less influenced by Axis I psychopathology, and thus potentially closer to a true picture of the personality. Sometimes, lengthy hospitalization brought out characteristics in patients that were not at first evident or were only suggested.

LEAD Conference

A LEAD diagnosis was the product of one or more group sessions focused on a single patient called the LEAD conference. Dr. Rosnick presided over these conferences and it was his responsibility to bring the group of clinicians to a consensus. In a straightforward case with less Axis II psychopathology or limited information available, a complete LEAD diagnosis could be agreed on in 1 to 1.5 hours. Patients who had features of many personality disorders or for whom the corroborating data were rich or complicated could take twice as long.

Diagnosis on gradient of severity. In the LEAD conference, each criterion for each DSM-III-R diagnosis was considered in turn. Because we began this work while DSM-III-R was in development, several versions of the DSM-III-R criteria were used. The LEAD data collection and the conference were conducted blind to the results of the initial research interview, no research psychiatrist who administered a structured interview participated in the LEAD, but the group knew which version of the DSM-III-R criteria were used in the interviews so that the same version would be applied during the LEAD.

We knew from the outset that the thresholds for most of the Axis II diagnoses were arbitrary. There was no strong empirical basis for including 9 criteria for one personality disorder or 7 for another. Likewise, whether 4, 5, or 6 should be the number present before a diagnosis was made was not empirically determined. Therefore, the final LEAD consensus diagnoses have always been expressed on a 4-point scale of severity ranging from 1, none or very few traits of a particular disorder; 2, some traits present; 3, sufficient traits present to almost meet DSM-III-R criteria; and 4, meets DSM-III-R criteria (Kass et al. 1985). This enabled us to be aware of near misses between the structured interviews and the LEAD and also to generate a personality profile on each patient, based on the LEAD, that included prominent personality traits and actual disorders.

Criteria on gradient of severity. As our experience with the LEAD

Table 3-2. Prevalence of Axis I disorders in patients admitted for long-term observation and treatment of personality disorders ($N = 30$)

DSM-III-R diagnostic class	n	Percentage
Mood disorders	27	90
Anxiety disorders	21	70
Eating disorders	7	23
Psychoactive substance use disorders	4	13
Psychotic disorders	2	7

conferences grew, we appreciated that the frequency or intensity with which a behavior or trait needed to be manifest for a particular criterion to be met was also a source of ambiguity. Therefore, we evolved our procedure to include a rating on each criterion for each disorder on a 5-point gradient of frequency with 0, never exhibits the behavior or trait; 1, almost never; 2, sometimes; 3, fairly often; and 4, very often. We then made a separate judgment of whether or not the person clinically met the criterion. This enabled us to view the frequencies differentially, because the number of times a person engaged in suicidal or self-mutilating behavior might be fewer to meet borderline personality disorder criterion no. 5 than the number of times a person's speech would need to be noted as excessively impressionistic or lacking in detail to meet histrionic personality disorder criterion no. 8.

Independent ratings and consensus. The most recent step in the development of our LEAD procedure has been to have every clinician participating in a conference complete his or her own rating form (rating each criterion for each disorder on the 5-point scale) before the conference. This will enable us to eventually test the reliability of longitudinal ratings of the behavior and traits of DSM-III-R personality disorders. A final consensus form continues to be the standard for comparison with the structured interviews.

Table 3-3 presents diagnostic criteria for borderline personality disorder as scored by consensus during a LEAD conference for one of the inpatients.

EXPERIENCE WITH LEAD AS VALIDITY STANDARD

Pilot Study

Our pilot study involved the first 20 patients who were admitted to the General Clinical Research Service and who remained hospitalized for the minimum period (6 weeks) we believed was necessary for a longitudinal assessment to be made. In this study (Skodol et al. 1988), we examined only the results of the SCID-II and their association to the LEAD diagnoses.

Among the important findings was that almost all patients had current Axis I disorders complicating the assessment of Axis II. Seventeen had mood disorders, 10 had anxiety disorders, 5 had eating disorders, and 4 had psychoactive substance use disorders.

On Axis II, results were mixed. Because we wanted to evaluate the SCID's ability to predict a longitudinal diagnosis, which we believe is inherently better than a diagnosis based on a single patient inter-

Table 3-3. Consensus ratings of criteria for borderline personality disorder from LEAD evaluation of sample patient

Borderline personality disorder[a]	Never	Almost never	Sometimes	Fairly often	Very often	Clinically meets criterion
1. Pattern of unstable and intense interpersonal relationships characterized by alternation between extremes of overidealization and devaluation	0	1	2	3	4	+ –
2. Impulsiveness in a least two areas that are potentially self-damaging, e.g., spending money, sex, substance use, shoplifting, reckless driving, binge eating. (Do not include suicidal or self-mutilating behavior covered in [5].)	0	1	2	3	4	+ –
3. Affective instability: marked shifts from baseline mood to depression, irritability, or anxiety, usually lasting a few hours and only rarely more than a few days	0	1	2	3	4	+ –
4. Inappropriate intense anger or lack of control of anger, e.g., frequent displays of temper, constant anger, recurrent physical fights	0	1	2	3	4	+ –

	0	1	2	3	4	+
5. Recurrent suicidal threats, gestures, or behavior, or self-mutilating behavior	0	1	2	3	4	+ / −
6. Marked and persistent identity disturbance manifested by uncertainty about at least two of the following: self-image, sexual orientation, long-term goals or career choice, type of friends desired, preferred values	0	1	2	3	4	+ / −
7. Chronic feelings of emptiness or boredom	0	1	2	3	4	+ / −
8. Frantic efforts to avoid real or imagined abandonment. (Do not include suicidal or self-mutilating behavior covered in [5].)	0	1	2	3	4	+ / −

Note. LEAD = longitudinal expert evaluation using all data. Numbers circled indicate ratings made on form during LEAD conference.
[a]Pervasive pattern of instability of mood, interpersonal relationships, and self-image beginning by early adulthood and present in various contexts as indicated by at least five criteria.

view, we examined the predictive power of the SCID for each personality disorder category. A test's predictive power is salient when the test is being used to select persons with a particular diagnosis for specialized treatment (Widiger et al. 1984), as is the case in our inpatient setting. In terms of overall diagnostic power, a measure of the total of correct positive tests and correct negative tests, the results in the pilot study ranged from a low of 0.45 (45% of test results were correct) for narcissistic personality disorder to a high of 0.95 (95% of test results correct) for antisocial personality disorder. The median diagnostic power was only 0.70, but five of the diagnoses generated by SCID-II (schizoid, schizotypal, antisocial, borderline, and dependent) had an overall diagnostic power value of 0.85 or better. Although suggestive that certain diagnoses may be adequately made by SCID-II, these predictive power rates are influenced by base rates of the disorders in the population. Few of our patients were diagnosed as schizoid and many were diagnosed as borderline; therefore, SCID was not adequately tested for these disorders in our population.

Considering our results as preliminary, we were nonetheless struck with the notion that diagnoses of disorders with distinctive psychopathology defined behaviorally (such as antisocial and schizotypal personality disorders) were more accurate than diagnoses of disorders whose items require more inference on the part of the interviewer, such as narcissistic and self-defeating personality disorders.

Comparison of Two Interviews

Our next step was in comparing the predictive powers of two interviews with divergent approaches to personality disorder diagnosis. At the time of this writing, we had collected 30 cases on whom we had both SCID and PDE interviews before admission and a LEAD diagnostic assessment based on a minimum of 6 weeks of inpatient hospitalization and observation.

This expanded sample (14 patients were part of the pilot report) was consistent with the pilot group in having a high proportion with current Axis I disorders. Ninety percent were diagnosed with a mood disorder and 70% with an anxiety disorder at the time of evaluation.

On Axis II, it became apparent that the two structured interviews did not diagnose each of the personality disorders at the same rate, nor did they diagnose the disorders at the same rate as the LEAD group. Table 3-4 presents the prevalences of individual DSM-III-R Axis II diagnoses by each of the three diagnostic methods. As can be seen from Table 4, paranoid and avoidant personality disorders are diagnosed more frequently by the SCID than by either the PDE or the LEAD; schizotypal and obsessive-compulsive personality disorders are diagnosed more frequently by the PDE than by the other two methods; and narcissistic and passive-aggressive personality disorders are diagnosed more by the LEAD than by either of the two structured interviews.

Over the three diagnostic methods, patients in this sample averaged four personality disorder diagnoses each. At least 66% received ≥ 3 diagnoses and at least 20% received ≥ 6 by each of the three methods. The finding that multiple personality disorder diagnoses are the rule, especially among patients with severe personality disorders, suggests that Axis II psychopathology might be more accurately measured dimensionally as opposed to categorically or that current Axis II disorders might be arranged in a hierarchy with less severe disorders subsumed under other more severe ones.

Table 3-5 shows the agreement between SCID and PDE for the 30 patients on each personality disorder diagnosis. Agreement is presented in terms of the kappa statistic which corrects for chance agreement that might occur if a disorder is especially common or uncommon in a particular sample. The kappas indicate acceptable

Table 3-4. Prevalence of DSM-III-R personality disorders by three diagnostic methods

	Method					
	SCID-II		PDE		LEAD	
Personality disorder	*n*	%	*n*	%	*n*	%
Paranoid	17	57	5	17	9	30
Schizoid	4	13	0	0	1	3
Schizotypal	4	13	8	27	4	13
Histrionic	7	23	4	13	9	30
Narcissistic	7	23	11	37	15	50
Antisocial	4	13	3	10	3	10
Borderline	20	67	22	73	24	80
Avoidant	20	67	15	50	9	30
Dependent	12	40	16	53	8	27
Obsessive-compulsive	8	27	11	37	3	10
Passive-aggressive	7	23	1	3	17	57
Self-defeating	13	43	8	27	14	47

Note. SCID-II = Structured Clinical Interview for DSM-III-R; PDE = Personality Disorder Examination; LEAD = longitudinal expert evaluation using all data.

agreement between the interviews for only narcissistic, antisocial, borderline, and obsessive-compulsive personality disorders.

In looking at the association between the structured interview assessments and the LEAD, we found that both interviews appear to diagnose certain disorders best; other disorders are not picked up that well by either interview (whether or not the interviews agree with each other). In general, SCID fares slightly better than PDE for all disorders diagnosed with reasonable accuracy (Skodol AE, Rosnick L, Kellman D, et al., unpublished observations).

Illustrations of Interview-LEAD Correspondence

To increase the reader's appreciation for the relationship of the results of the structured interviews to the LEAD diagnoses, a series of case vignettes follows. Details of comorbid Axis I disorders that were prevalent (Oldham JM, Skodol AE, Kellman D, et al., unpublished observations) were omitted from the vignettes to keep them brief and focus attention on Axis II psychopathology. In some cases the structured interviews appeared to be adequate, using the LEAD diagnoses as the criterion. This could be the case whether the person being studied had many or few Axis II diagnoses. The first two vignettes describe patients whose SCID-II and PDE assessments were substantiated by the LEAD evaluation.

Table 3-5.   Agreement between Structured Clinical Interview for DSM-III-R Personality Disorders (SCID-II) and Personality Disorder Examination (PDE)

Personality disorder	Kappa
Paranoid	0.27
Schizoid	0
Schizotypal	0.39
Histrionic	0.45
Narcissistic	0.53
Antisocial	0.52
Borderline	0.53
Avoidant	0.40
Dependent	0.47
Obsessive-compulsive	0.77
Passive-aggressive	0.20
Self-defeating	0.36

Case Vignette 1. A 24-year-old single unemployed homeless man was transferred from a nearby state hospital for treatment of dysthymic disorder and borderline personality. His chief complaint was "I screwed up a lot."

The man described himself as a troublemaker since age 9 when, in the context of his parents' separation, he was disruptive and delinquent. He dropped out of high school despite having what he called "a good brain." He was dishonorably discharged from the army a few months before the end of his tour of duty, and he left a drug rehabilitation program 1 month before completion. He impulsively quit jobs whenever he had enough money "to get by for awhile." In the years before admission he had no stable living arrangement. He traveled from state to state, usually fleeing financial or other obligations. He was arrested and charged with breaking and entering by his own grandmother who eventually dropped the charges. He reported having lived on the streets on several occasions after having been kicked out of supervised housing and having been rejected by his mother and by men's shelters whose rules he previously had violated. The man stated that he had had no close friends since childhood. He sabotaged all of his relationships by lying, stealing, or exploiting his friends. He experienced chronic unhappiness, characterized by guilt over failures. He was very self-critical, especially over his tendency to hurt people. He described himself as "obnoxious, rebellious, dishonest, immature, and irresponsible." He made two suicidal gestures that precipitated admissions to the state hospital. He described these as acts of desperation and manipulation to obtain shelter. He acknowledged a long history of drug abuse.

Results of structured interviews indicated the patient met or was very near to meeting the criteria for many personality disorders. The two interviews agreed that the patient had all four cluster B disorders, i.e., antisocial, borderline, histrionic, and narcissistic. The SCID also made the diagnoses of paranoid, passive-aggressive, and self-defeating personality disorders, and the PDE added dependent. For three of four additional diagnoses, the other interview indicated that the patient fell only one criterion short of receiving the diagnosis; for the remaining one (SCID passive-aggressive), the patient met three of the five required criteria.

After 3 months of hospitalization, the patient had a LEAD evaluation. The LEAD confirmed the presence of the seven diagnoses made on the SCID-II. The only diagnosis made by either structured interview that was not confirmed was PDE dependency. No diagnosis was made by the LEAD that had not been made by the SCID.

Case Vignette 2. A 20-year-old single woman requested long-term hospitalization following 2 years of repeated drug overdoses and self-inflicted stab wounds. Previously, she had 10 brief psychiatric hospitalizations, but had never continued inpatient or outpatient treatment for more than several weeks.

Although successful in school and athletics until age 18, the young woman had always harbored a deep sense of inferiority, resentment, and isolation. She described feeling a need to punish someone but she did not know whom. She would experience irresistible urges to take pills or to stab, cut, or inflict bruises on herself. She would carefully plan and methodically carry out acts of self-mutilation; afterwards she would report to the police that someone had done them to her. On one occasion, she stabbed herself in the abdomen 32 times with a scalpel over a period of several hours while walking around her community before going to an emergency room with significant blood loss. The patient also had frequent episodes of binge eating and laxative abuse during this 2-year period.

Although this woman had obvious character pathology, neither PDE nor SCID assessments of Axis II indicated that she met criteria for any specific DSM-III-R personality disorder. However, she was noted to be subthreshold for borderline personality disorder (meeting four of five required criteria) on the SCID and met three criteria for borderline and four for narcissistic on the PDE.

The patient's hospital course was characterized by sullen anger, self-destructive behavior, and defiant attempts to control her treatment and render it ineffective. She took an overdose of diet pills she had hidden in her belongings. Although on constant observation, she concealed her arms beneath a large book on her lap and painstakingly carved her therapist's name with an emphatic "no" before it into her forearm with a knitting needle that she had obtained from another patient. She tried to pressure the staff into taking her off constant observation, threatening that she would refuse to speak until they did so. She remained on constant observation for several months until her anger, defiance, and self-destructive urges subsided.

On the LEAD evaluation the only DSM-III-R personality disorder diagnosis for which she met criteria was borderline personality disorder. Symptoms that were elicited or suspected during the structured interviews that were confirmed by the LEAD included impulsiveness, recurrent suicidal threats, identity disturbance, and chronic feelings of emptiness or boredom. The main difference between the interview and the LEAD results, which accounted for the patient receiving a diagnosis of borderline personality disorder on the LEAD, was the judgment that she developed unstable intense relationships with ward staff, characterized by "splitting."

Occasionally, the results of the structured interviews appeared to be out of line with the LEAD assessment. Sometimes the interviews yielded many false-positive diagnoses that could not be confirmed by longitudinal observation. The next vignette illustrates the problem.

Case Vignette 3. Long-term hospital treatment of atypical depression and borderline personality disorder was recommended for a 32-year-old single man. Before admission he had been living alone and working as an editor for a book publisher.

The patient dates the onset of his problems to 1981 when he began experiencing numbness and tingling in his right hand that soon spread to his legs. Over the next few months, he experienced additional somatic symptoms that he attributed to various medications that he had been given. According to the patient, one caused him to experience "unbridled anxiety as if the lid was off," another to feel "spacey with a stuffy feeling in my head" as though his eyes were "placed in unusual positions" on his face, and a third caused "every nerve ending in my head to begin to explode." He experienced compulsions to tap furniture with his right hand and to pace and run up and down stairs for hours at a time. Because of this hyperactivity he missed 4 months of work and entered a psychiatric hospital for the first time.

In the hospital he had his first pseudoseizure, which was characterized by collapsing and having spasms of his arms and legs. The patient's symptoms rapidly disappeared after he was told by a consultant that he would have to "rise above it all or he would end up in a state hospital." Two years later his pacing and compulsions recurred. He began to experience excruciating "mental pain" behind his eyes and a slowing of his mental processes. The patient was rehospitalized after he had stuck a steel nail file into an electrical socket in a suicide attempt.

The following year the patient claimed he felt more irritable, erratic, somewhat paranoid, and less sociable. He experienced depersonalization. He started acting out certain roles in front of a mirror, i.e., pretending that he was an emperor, his mother, or the Messiah. When he could no longer tolerate his suspiciousness and recurrent depersonalization, he checked himself into the psychiatric hospital from which he was later transferred to a private psychiatric facility.

On the evaluation day, this patient received 8 personality disorder diagnoses according to the PDE and all 11 diagnoses according to the SCID-II. He was one criterion short on the three diagnoses not made by PDE: schizoid, histrionic, and self-defeating.

On admission, the man appeared guarded and anxious. His speech was circumstantial. He was noted to be overweight, stoop shouldered, disheveled, and suffering from severe facial acne. He was described as clinging.

Multiple previous psychiatrists had described significant character pathology. He had been noted to be guarded, suspicious, angry, dependent, unstable, intolerant of being alone, shy, a loner, obsessive in his thinking, and compulsive in his behavior. The patient reported that he had no activities that he enjoyed. He saw himself as "a sensitive person who lets people push me around and step on me. I need a lot of affection, but I never got it. I am too dependent on my mother. I am not sure if I could cope with it if she would die today."

According to the LEAD, the patient only met criteria for schizotypal, passive-aggressive, and self-defeating personality disorders. However, he was noted to have significant traits of schizoid, borderline, avoidant, and obsessive-compulsive disorders. The LEAD was based on a brief hospitalization (7 weeks) and it was noted that the patient's prominent social isolation and passivity made it difficult for staff to form strong opinions about other aspects of his personality.

The opposite situation also occurred. A few patients seemed not to have any personality disorder or few when assessed at a single point in time, but after spending a period of time under observation on the unit, significant psychopathology could be observed. The next case is an example of one in which the interviews seemed to yield a preponderantly false-negative assessment of personality psychopathology that might be more readily observed than revealed by direct questioning.

Case Vignette 4. A 21-year-old single man was admitted for long-term inpatient treatment of refractory depression and severe character pathology. He had a history of poor social, behavioral, and academic functioning dating from childhood. With much difficulty he managed to complete high school and enroll in college. After a week, he returned home complaining of increasing anxiety and depression. On treatment with medication, his depression resolved. He resumed college and appeared to do well for a few months, but then experienced a recurrence of depression with panic attacks at the time of final examinations.

During the next 5 months he was treated with various different antidepressants that either caused significant side effects or from which he derived only transient benefit. When he was unable to tolerate a day program, he became increasingly agitated and depressed. He took an overdose of antidepressants, which resulted in his first psychiatric hospitalization. One day after admission he reported no longer feeling suicidal. After 1 month in the hospital his depression remitted. A few weeks after his discharge the depression recurred and he was admitted for long-term treatment.

The PDE assessment revealed no personality disorder, although there were almost enough symptoms for diagnoses of borderline and avoidant personality disorders. SCID-II indicated threshold diagnoses of avoidant and dependent personality disorders and subthreshold borderline.

The patient received a LEAD evaluation 8 months after admission. By the LEAD, staff agreed that the patient met criteria for borderline, histrionic, narcissistic, dependent, passive-aggressive, and self-defeating personality disorders.

A comparison of LEAD observations with interview assessments of histrionic, narcissistic, and passive-aggressive personality disorders was revealing. The patient was observed during hospitalization to have constantly sought approval from others, expressed emotion with inappropriate exaggeration, experienced discomfort when not the center of attention, displayed rapidly shifting and shallow emotions, and acted in a self-centered way with no frustration tolerance. He was also observed to meet all nine DSM-III-R criteria for narcissistic personality disorder. It was especially evident that he had extreme contempt for the staff and the treatment program. He insisted that only expert consultants whom he had chosen could possibly suggest a treatment plan for him that he had not already considered himself. During activities and general community affairs, he displayed characteristic features of passive-aggressive personality disorder. When initially seen by research psychiatrists, the patient acknowledged sufficient symptoms to meet only one criterion of narcissistic personality disorder, none of either histrionic or passive-aggressive during the PDE, only two criteria for narcissistic and histrionic, and one for passive-aggressive via the SCID-II.

The LEAD proved to be valuable in deciding which interview assessment was more accurate in cases where the interview results diverged from each other. Of the 13 cases in which the interviews can be said to have significantly diverged, the LEAD was closer to SCID than PDE in eight cases. The last vignette is an example of such a case.

Case Vignette 5. Life-long depression and extreme social isolation plagued a 37-year-old single woman. Her mother remembered her as a very quiet, painfully shy, solemn child. She preferred to play alone and remembered having only one girlfriend in all her school years.

School was "a torture," she said, "because I had to interact with other people." Classmates teased her by asking each other, "Can she talk?" Although quite young, she resolved never to marry and have children. In contrast to her socially impoverished real life, her fantasy life was rich with adventure, romance, and close human relationships.

The patient believed in extrasensory perception and reincarnation. She felt she was paying in this life for sins committed in another life. She sought the help of numerous fortune tellers, faith healers, and hypnotists to solve these mysteries, but none could help her. She felt the presence of spiritual beings and had the illusion of seeing faces.

Since childhood she had been unable to trust others for fear of being ridiculed by them, a fear that often caused her to sweat and shiver when watched by others. She developed severe social phobia, agoraphobia, and panic attacks. She lost many secretarial jobs because of her extreme anxiety toward others and had not worked in 3 years. She lived alone in an apartment for 6 years before moving back with her parents at age 27. The first of two suicide attempts occurred after her first and only boyfriend broke up with her after their first and only sexual encounter.

The PDE evaluation indicated diagnoses of paranoid, schizotypal, borderline, avoidant, and obsessive-compulsive personality disorders. The SCID-II agreed with paranoid, schizotypal, and avoidant, but found only modest evidence of borderline and obsessive-compulsive disorders. SCID-II added a diagnosis of schizoid personality disorder.

The LEAD was based on a period of inpatient observation of almost 1 year. The LEAD agreed with the SCID assessment. The only borderline characteristic observed was identity disturbance.

PROBLEMS WITH THE LEAD AS A STANDARD

Although our initial experiences with the LEAD have convinced us of its potential value as a validating criterion for structured assessments of Axis II, it is also clear that further research is needed before the LEAD can be used with confidence.

First, the reliability of LEAD-type evaluations has not been established. Unless it can be demonstrated that longitudinal assessments incorporated into the LEAD can be made reliably, a significant factor accounting for the lack of a relationship between a structured interview diagnosis and a LEAD diagnosis might be the variation in the LEAD ratings. As mentioned previously, a study to test the reliability of the LEAD has been started.

Second, the LEAD procedure follows a criterion by criterion, disorder by disorder approach similar to the SCID. Therefore, the better correspondence between the SCID and LEAD might be due to a bias in the structure of the LEAD reporting. It is possible to conceive of the LEAD as a randomly arranged listing of all the DSM-III-R criteria for personality disorders, similar in construction to self-report scales. This arrangement would reduce the halo effect during the LEAD of raters knowing whether a patient is meeting the criteria for a given disorder or is close to meeting the criteria. However, it seems to us that this is not clinically realistic. A clinical diagnostician is seeking patterns of symptoms that correspond to a recognizable syndrome. Noticing several together, the diagnostician evaluates other related signs or symptoms and makes the suspected diagnosis or rules it out and investigates another alternative. To eliminate cues to pattern recognition by randomly arranging signs and symptoms would be equivalent to examining different parts of the body and its functioning randomly. It seems to us that this would result in poorer diagnostic acumen.

Third, disagreements between structured interview and longitudinal diagnoses may be a matter of degree. Both methods as used in our studies require that a diagnosis be made on the basis of the fixed (and for the most part arbitrary) number of diagnostic criteria met, as specified in DSM-III-R. It is possible that a more flexible approach to diagnosis or to the examination of agreement would lead to fewer discrepancies.

Finally, observation of a patient during an inpatient hospitalization may not be representative of real life. This may be especially true when the unit's structure inevitably frustrates some of the patient's wishes that might be gratified outside of the hospital. Nonetheless, we believe that inpatient observations supplemented by history and interviews with individuals who are part of the patient's life can potentially yield an accurate picture of personality functioning. Furthermore, we can think of no more convenient way of collecting day-to-day observations of a patient other than in an inpatient setting.

Any other periodic evaluations would also run the risk of being nonrepresentative samples of behavior.

In conclusion, the LEAD appears promising as a standard for validating Axis II diagnoses. We hope that other research groups will attempt to use it.

REFERENCES

American Psychiatric Association: Diagnostic and Statistical Manual of Mental Disorders, 3rd Edition. Washington, DC, American Psychiatric Association, 1980

American Psychiatric Association: Diagnostic and Statistical Manual of Mental Disorders, 3rd Edition, Revised. Washington, DC, American Psychiatric Association, 1987

Blashfield RK, McElroy RA: The 1985 journal literature on the personality disorders. Compr Psychiatry 28:536–546, 1987

Blashfield RK, McElroy RA: Ontology of personality disorder categories. Psychiatric Annals 19:126–131, 1989

Campbell D, Fiske D: Convergent and discriminant validation by the multi-trait-multimethod matrix. Psychol Bull 56:81–105, 1959

Cloninger CR: A systematic method for clinical description and classification of personality variants. Arch Gen Psychiatry 44:513–588, 1987

Cronbach LJ, Meehl PE: Construct validity in psychological tests. Psychol Bull 52:281–302, 1955

Endicott J, Spitzer RL: A diagnostic interview: the Schedule for Affective Disorders and Schizophrenia. Arch Gen Psychiatry 35:837–844, 1978

Feighner JP, Robins E, Guze SB, et al: Diagnostic criteria for use in psychiatric research. Arch Gen Psychiatry 26:57–63, 1972

Frances AJ, Widiger TA: Personality disorders, in An Annotated Bibliography of DSM-III. Edited by Skodol AE, Spitzer RL. Washington, DC, American Psychiatric Press, 1987, pp 125–133

Grunhaus L, King D, Greden JF, et al: Depression and panic in patients with borderline personality disorder. Biol Psychiatry 20:688–692, 1985

Hasin DS, Skodol AE: Standardized diagnostic interviews for psychiatric research, in The Instruments of Psychiatric Research. Edited by Thompson C. London, John Wiley, 1989, pp 19–57

Hudson JI, Pope HG Jr, Jonas JM, et al: Phenomenologic relationship of eating disorders to major affective disorders. Psychiatry Res 9:345–354, 1983

Hyler SE, Frances A: Clinical implications of Axis I–Axis II interactions. Compr Psychiatry 26:345–351, 1985

Hyler S, Rieder R, Spitzer R, et al: The Personality Diagnostic Questionnaire Revised (PDQ-R). New York, New York State Psychiatric Institute, 1987

Hyler S, Rieder R, Williams J, et al: The Personality Diagnostic Questionnaire: development and preliminary results. J Pers Disord 2:229–237, 1988

Kass F, Skodol AE, Charles E, et al: Scaled ratings of DSM-III personality disorders. Am J Psychiatry 142:627–630, 1985

Kernberg OF: Severe Personality Disorders: Psychotherapeutic Strategies. New Haven, CT, Yale University Press, 1984

Khantzian EJ, Treece C: DSM-III psychiatric diagnosis of narcotics addicts: recent findings. Arch Gen Psychiatry 42:1067–1071, 1985

Kosten TR, Rounsaville BJ, Kleber HD: DSM-III personality disorders in opiate addicts. Compr Psychiatry 23:572–581, 1982

Levin AP, Hyler SE: DSM-III personality diagnosis in bulimia. Compr Psychiatry 27:47–53, 1986

Loranger A, Susman V, Oldham J, et al: Personality Disorder Examination. White Plains, NY, New York Hospital–Cornell Medical Center Westchester Division, 1985

Loranger AW, Susman V, Oldham J, et al: The Personality Disorder Examination: a preliminary report. J Pers Disord 1:1–13, 1987

McGlashan TH: The borderline syndrome, II: is it a variant of schizophrenia or affective syndrome? Arch Gen Psychiatry 40:1319–1323, 1983

Mellsop G, Varghese F, Joshua S, et al: The reliability of Axis II of DSM-III. Am J Psychiatry 139:1360–1361, 1982

Millon T: The MCMI provides a good assessment of DSM-III disorders: the MCMI-II will prove even better. J Pers Assess 49:379–391, 1985

Morey L, Waugh M, Blashfield R: MMPI scales for DSM-III personality disorders: their derivation and correlates. J Pers Assess 49:245–251, 1985

Pilkonis PA, Frank E: Personality pathology in recurrent depression: nature, prevalence, and relationship to treatment response. Am J Psychiatry 145:435–441, 1988

Pope HG Jr, Jonas JM, Hudson JI, et al: The validity of DSM-III borderline personality disorder: a phenomenologic, family history, treatment response, and long-term follow-up study. Arch Gen Psychiatry 40:23–30, 1983

Reich JH: DSM-III personality disorders and the outcome of treated panic disorder. Am J Psychiatry 145:1149–1152, 1988

Robins E, Guze S: Establishment of diagnostic validity in psychiatric illness: its application to schizophrenia. Am J Psychiatry 126:983–987, 1970

Robins LN, Helzer JE, Croughan J, et al: National Institute of Mental Health Diagnostic Interview Schedule: its history, characteristics, and validity. Arch Gen Psychiatry 38:381–389, 1981

Rosnick L: Use of a long-term inpatient unit as a site for learning psychotherapy. Psychiatr Clin North Am 10:309–323, 1987

Schuckit MA: The clinical implications of primary diagnostic groups among alcoholics. Arch Gen Psychiatry 42:1043–1049, 1985

Skodol AE: Problems in Differential Diagnosis: From DSM-III to DSM-III-R in Clinical Practice. Washington, DC, American Psychiatric Press, 1989

Skodol AE, Spitzer RL: The development of reliable diagnostic criteria in psychiatry. Ann Rev Med 33:317–326, 1982

Skodol AE, Rosnick L, Kellman D, et al: Validating structured DSM-III-R personality disorder assessments with longitudinal data. Am J Psychiatry 145:1297–1299, 1988

Spitzer RL: Psychiatric diagnosis: are clinicians still necessary? Compr Psychiatry 24:399–411, 1983

Spitzer RL, Endicott J, Robins E: Clinical criteria for psychiatric diagnosis and DSM-III. Am J Psychiatry 132:1187–1192, 1975

Spitzer RL, Endicott J, Robins E: Research Diagnostic Criteria: rationale and reliability. Arch Gen Psychiatry 35:773–789, 1978

Spitzer RL, Forman JB, Nee J: DSM-III field trials, I: initial interrater reliability. Am J Psychiatry 136:815–817, 1979

Spitzer RL, Williams JBW, Gibbon M: The Structured Clinical Interview for DSM-III-R Personality Disorders (SCID-II, 3/1/87). New York, Biometrics Research Department, New York State Psychiatric Institute, 1987a

Spitzer RL, Williams JBW, Gibbon M: Structured Clinical Interview for DSM-III-R, Patient Version. New York, Biometrics Research Department, New York State Psychiatric Institute, 1987b

Stangl D, Pfohl B, Zimmerman M, et al: A structured interview for the DSM-III personality disorders. Arch Gen Psychiatry 42:591–596, 1985

Van Valkenberg CH, Akiskal HS, Puzantian V, et al: Anxious depressions: clinical, family history, and naturalistic outcome comparisons with panic and major depressive disorders. J Affective Disord 6:67–82, 1984

Widiger TA, Frances A: Interviews and inventories for the measurement of personality disorders. Clin Psychol Rev 7:49–75, 1987

Widiger TA, Hurt SW, Frances A, et al: Diagnostic efficiency and DSM-III. Arch Gen Psychiatry 41:1005–1012, 1984

Widiger T, Frances A, Warner L, et al: Diagnostic criteria for the borderline and schizotypal personality disorders. J Abnorm Psychol 95:43–51, 1986

Wing JK, Birley JLT, Cooper JE, et al: Reliability of a procedure for measuring and classifying present psychiatric state. Br J Psychiatry 113:499–515, 1967

Chapter 4

Biologic Validators of Personality Disorders

Richard J. Kavoussi, M.D.
Larry J. Siever, M.D.

Chapter 4

Biologic Validators of Personality Disorders

Traditionally, psychiatric disorders have been defined by developing behavioral criteria that appear to separate the disorder from other psychiatric disorders. Attempts are then made to externally validate the disorder through the use of family studies, biologic markers, clinical course, treatment response, and outcome (Robins and Guze 1970). Biologic markers have been widely used in attempts to validate Axis I disorders. For example, it has been suggested that lack of cortisol suppression by dexamethasone may be a marker for endogenous depressions (Carroll et al. 1981); lactate infusions have been shown to induce panic-like symptoms in patients with anxiety disorders (Cowley et al. 1987); and smooth-pursuit eye tracking has been found to be impaired in schizophrenic individuals (Holzman et al. 1974).

This approach offers several advantages. The use of categorical models is consistent with medical models of illness and past and current terminology used by clinicians. Standard operationalized criteria (e.g., DSM-III [American Psychiatric Association 1980] and Research Diagnostic Criteria) can be used to define disorders for which studies of biologic markers can be conducted. This allows for comparison of results of biologic tests over time and from setting to setting. The biologic marker approach to validating psychiatric disorders also could be used to define specific subgroups of disorders with similar underlying pathophysiology. This would allow investigators to make hypotheses about potential somatic treatments for these subgroups based on the particular biologic abnormality found. Although not yet realized, biologic marker studies also offer the potential advantage of providing an opportunity to correlate findings with results of studies of other markers/validators (e.g., family history studies, twin studies, genetic linkage studies).

This strategy, in which diagnostic criteria are formulated on the basis of clinical phenomenology and attempts are made to correlate biologic markers with each disorder, has only recently been applied to personality psychopathology. As with Axis I disorders, such a strategy has the advantage of using standardized operationalized criteria for specific personality disorders (so that results can be compared from study to study) and consistency with current clinical terminology.

However, validating categorical personality disorders with any external validator poses several problems. There have been problems in defining the criteria sets for personality disorders. This is reflected in the overlap among personality disorders (Pfohl et al. 1986; Widiger et al. 1988) which makes it difficult to study biologic indices in homogeneous samples. Even when structured interviews are used to make personality diagnoses, inadequacies in the criteria and their measurement are such that the choice of instrument may influence the outcome of the study (Kavoussi et al. 1989b). Thus, current personality disorder classifications define heterogeneous populations and studies of biologic markers in these disorders may show conflicting results depending on the nature of the sample studied.

Compatible with the high degree of overlap among personality disorders is evidence that personality psychopathology does not necessarily occur as discrete categorical diagnoses. It has been argued that dimensional models would better characterize personality psychopathology as occurring on a continuum with normal personality traits (Frances 1982; Widiger et al. 1987). Many dimensional models have been proposed in the past to explore character disturbances, e.g., the Minnesota Multiphasic Personality Inventory (MMPI) scales and personality clusters of DSM-III-R (eccentric, dramatic, and anxious) (American Psychiatric Association 1987). Widiger derived a multidimensional scaling of personality disorders including degree of assertion, degree of social involvement, and anxious rumination versus acting out. Such models suggest that we attempt to correlate available biologic data with a particular dimension. Unfortunately, there has been little empirical research to externally validate these dimensional models, and studies that have been conducted in this area have been offshoots of studies of Axis I disorders, providing little guidance in the investigation of dimensional models of psychopathology. Yet the use of dimensional classifications in biologic studies offer an advantage in that gradations of measured psychopathology and symptom clusters can often be more easily correlated with biologic measures than can categorical diagnoses.

Another noncategorical approach suited to the study of biologic markers in personality disorders is to consider these disorders as prototypes or a form fruste of particular Axis I disorders on a spectrum of psychopathology with similar underlying biologic substrates and genetic antecedents but with differing degrees of phenomenologic expression due to environmental or developmental factors (Siever et al. 1985). The personality disorders may represent a common albeit milder form of the disorder than the parent Axis I disorder. For example, schizotypal personality may occur on a genetic continuum of schizophrenia-related illnesses (Kendler et al. 1981). Preliminary studies have found similar abnormalities in both schizophrenia and schizotypal personality disorder: impaired smooth-pursuit eye movements, increased ventricle-to-brain ratio, abnormal dopaminergic functioning (Siever 1985), and treatment response to neuroleptics (Hymowitz et al. 1986). Similarly, the affective lability and dysregulation seen in borderline personality disorder may occur on a biologically mediated spectrum with other disorders of mood (dysthymia, cyclothymia, hypomania, and bipolar illness) (Akiskal 1981), whereas avoidant personality disorder may represent a mild expression of the psychophysiologic abnormalities that contribute to anxiety disorders.

Our aim in this chapter will be to define several spectra of personality psychopathology that could be correlated with biologic markers, review current evidence in this area, and highlight future areas for investigation. We hypothesize four dimensions to investigate: 1) cognitive-perceptual organization, 2) affective regulation, 3) impulse control, and 4) anxiety/social inhibition.

COGNITIVE-PERCEPTUAL ORGANIZATION

Disturbances in the ability to cognitively process information from internal and external stimuli are often seen in personality disordered patients. These difficulties result in perceptual aberrations in several spheres: misperception of environmental cues (illusions), misperception of internal cues (somatization), misperception of interpersonal cues (social anxiety and isolation), and misperception of cognitive cues (magical thinking, ideas of reference, paranoia). These problems are commonly observed in schizophrenic patients and in attenuated form in personality disorders now grouped in the odd cluster in DSM-III-R: schizotypal, schizoid, and paranoid. Schizophrenic patients have been found to perform abnormally on various tasks of information processing (smooth-pursuit eye movements, continuous performance tasks, backward masking), and preliminary evidence suggests that personality disordered patients with problems in the cognitive-perceptual sphere have similar deficits.

Abnormalities in smooth-pursuit eye movements (ability to track a smoothly moving target) may reflect disrupted neurointegrative functioning of the frontal lobes and have been found to be abnormal in both acute and remitted schizophrenic patients (Holzman et al. 1974) and are not a function of neuroleptic medications. Disturbances in smooth pursuit have been correlated with schizotypal symptoms in college volunteers and appear to be more specific for negative schizotypal symptoms (social anxiety, isolation, impoverished speech) than for positive schizotypal symptoms (magical thinking, illusions, ideas of reference) (Siever et al. 1984).

Another test of neurointegrative functioning is backward masking, a process in which a visual stimulus is rapidly followed by another visual stimulus and the subject is asked to identify the original stimulus. Schizophrenic and schizotypal patients have been found to have impaired responses to these tasks (Braff 1981). College volunteers with MMPI profiles similar to those found in schizophrenia are also more likely to show impairment in backward masking tasks than matched control subjects (Merritt and Balogh 1984).

Continuous performance tasks involve having an individual monitor a rapidly changing display of letters and respond to a predetermined combination of letters. Schizophrenic patients have been found to have decreased response times on these tasks (Nuechterlein et al. 1986) and, as in the case of backward masking, college volunteers with schizotypal-like MMPI patterns also have been found to have impairments on this task (Nuechterlein 1987). There is also preliminary evidence from our group that a subgroup of schizotypal patients may show an increased ventricle-to-brain ratio and disturbed conformation of the P300 wave in auditory evoked potentials that is intermediate between that found in schizophrenic subjects and healthy control subjects.

Dopaminergic dysfunction as measured by cerebrospinal fluid and plasma levels of the dopamine metabolite homovanillic acid (HVA) have been found to correlate with psychotic symptoms in schizophrenia (Davidson and Davis 1988), and changes in plasma HVA have been associated with therapeutic response to neuroleptics (Davila et al. 1988). A similar relationship has been found between dopamine activity and psychotic-like symptoms in schizotypal personality disorder (Kavoussi et al. 1989a). Patients meeting DSM-III-R criteria for schizotypal personality disorder were found to have significantly higher mean levels of plasma HVA than healthy control subjects or patients with other personality disorders. In addition, plasma HVA significantly correlated with psychotic-like schizotypal traits (magical thinking, ideas of reference, illusions) but not with negative traits (inadequate rapport and social isolation). These results suggest that schizotypal traits in personality disordered patients share similar biologic antecedents with schizophrenic symptoms (neurointegrative dysfunction and dopamine dysfunction). Based on preliminary evidence it may also be hypothesized that dopaminergic dysfunctions (as reflected in dopamine metabolite measurements) are associated with positive psychotic-like symptoms or traits and that neurointegrative dysfunctions (as reflected in information processing tasks) correlate with negative deficit symptoms in schizophrenic spectrum disorders. Future studies are needed to test these hypotheses.

AFFECTIVE REGULATION

Individuals with personality disorders often exhibit intensely experienced, rapidly shifting affective states (guilt, sadness, and anger). Affective states in these patients are often exquisitely sensitive to events in the environment such as rejection, criticism, or frustration, frequently out of proportion to the external stimuli that elicited the change in affect. Disturbances in this spectrum may manifest themselves in the shifting and environmentally sensitive affective states described in patients with borderline, narcissistic, and histrionic personality disorders.

The dexamethasone suppression test, the thyrotropin-releasing hormone test, and EEG sleep studies have been widely used in investigations of biologic markers of affective disorders. These tests have also been examined in patients diagnosed with borderline personality disorder, with many patients showing nonsuppression of cortisol in response to dexamethasone (Beeber et al. 1984; Krishman et al. 1984; Soloff et al. 1982; Steele 1983; Sternbach et al. 1983), a blunted thyrotropin-stimulating hormone response to thyrotropin-releasing hormone (Garbutt et al. 1983; Sternbach et al. 1983), and decreased rapid eye movement latency (Bell et al. 1983; McNamara et al. 1984). However, it is unclear whether these tests are assessing the affective dysregulation described previously, a coexisting Axis I affective disorder, or some other variable.

Because central nervous system stimulants are known to produce elevations in mood in healthy subjects, it is natural to study the effect of stimulants (i.e., amphetamine or methylphenidate) on abnormalities in affective regulation. Unfortunately, challenges of intravenous amphetamine or methylphenidate in borderline patients have produced conflicting results. Although some studies have noted marked dysphoria in response to the stimulant challenge (Lucas et al. 1987), others have reported improvement in mood (Schulz et al. 1988). Interestingly, the latter study found that patients meeting criteria for borderline personality only showed improvement in mood, whereas patients with both borderline and schizotypal symptoms had negative reactions to the challenge (dysphoria and increased psychosis). This suggests that the stimulant may improve the affective component of these personality disorders but may worsen those symptoms in the cognitive-perceptual spectrum (presumably involving the dopaminergic system). However, larger samples replicating these findings are required.

Cholinergic mechanisms may also play a role in the regulation of affect. Challenges with cholinergic agents such as physostigmine produce depressive symptoms in patients with major Axis I affective disorders at lower doses than in healthy control subjects (Janowsky et al. 1981). Bipolar patients have been found to be more sensitive than control subjects to the decrease in rapid eye movement sleep latency produced by the muscarinic agonist arecoline (Nurnberger et al. 1989), and similar findings have been reported for borderline personality disorder (Bell et al. 1983). Because cholinergic supersensitivity appears to be involved in affective dysregulation in Axis I disorders, it is reasonable to hypothesize that cholinergic dysfunction might also underlie the affective instability often seen in personality disorders. This hypothesis must be tested further by performing cholinergic challenge studies in patients suffering from affective lability.

IMPULSE CONTROL

Individuals with personality psychopathology often exhibit disturbances in modulation of frustration tolerance and inhibition of impulses. These individuals have a lower threshold to internal (e.g., affective states) or external (e.g., criticism, rejection, praise) stimuli leading to a tendency to act out against themselves or others without regard to aversive consequences. This disturbance can be conceptualized as occurring on a continuum with disorders of impulse control on Axis I (e.g., substance abuse, compulsive gambling, bulimia, intermittent explosive disorder). Among current personality disorders, this behavioral dimension is most often seen in personality disorders in the "dramatic" cluster of DSM-III-R: histrionic, borderline, and antisocial personalities. In these patients the disinhibition of impulses may lead to recurrent bouts of aggressive behavior, recurrent suicidal or self-mutilating behavior, and disturbances in interpersonal relationships.

Data from preclinical and clinical studies suggest that these traits may be associated with disturbances in central serotonergic neurotransmission. For example, lesions of the serotonergic system in animals result in behavioral disinhibition and aggression even in the face of aversive stimuli (Valzelli 1981). Aggressive and suicidal behaviors in personality disordered patients have been shown to correlate inversely with cerebrospinal fluid levels of 5-hydroxyindoleacetic acid, the major metabolite of serotonin (Brown et al. 1982). Lower levels of cerebrospinal fluid 5-hydroxyindoleacetic acid have also been related to impulsive firesetting (Virkkunen et al. 1987) and outwardly directed hostility in healthy control subjects (Roy et al. 1988). Imipramine binding in the central nervous system, which has been correlated with central serotonergic activity (Langer et al. 1981), has been found to be decreased in the prefrontal cortex of victims of suicide (Stanley et al. 1982). Increases in postsynaptic serotonin receptors have been found in the brains of suicide victims (Mann et al. 1986), again suggesting a role for serotonin in the mediation of self-destructive behaviors.

Challenge studies have also provided evidence that central serotonergic activity is reduced in patients with disinhibition of impulse control. Measures of physical aggression, irritability, and suicidality have been found to correlate with decreased release of prolactin from the hypothalamus in response to the central serotonin releaser fenfluramine in personality disordered patients (Coccaro et al. 1989). A similar response has been found when personality disordered patients are challenged with *m*-chlorophenylpiperazine, a direct serotonin agonist (Coccaro, in press). Medication trials have also been consistent with this hypothesis with lithium, having partial serotonergic properties, demonstrating efficacy in decreasing irritable acting-out behavior (Sheard et al. 1976; Wickham and Reed 1987). These studies clearly implicate serotonergic subsensitivity in the genesis of impulsive behaviors (both aggressive and self-destructive).

ANXIETY/SOCIAL INHIBITION

Individuals with personality disorders commonly report excessive anxiety (situational or global) in response to environmental or internal stimuli that would not be anxiety provoking to most people. Anxiety in turn leads to inhibition of responsiveness which produces the behavioral abnormalities seen in these patients. Thus, fear of criticism or embarrassment may lead to avoidance of relationships (as in avoidant personality disorder). Similarly, fear of separation may lead to difficulties in making simple decisions without others and in being assertive (as in dependent personality disorder).

Unfortunately, although ubiquitous to many personality disorders, there have been few empirical studies of biologic factors underlying anxiety traits on Axis II. Noradrenergic mechanisms have been implicated in the genesis of certain Axis I anxiety disorders. For example, yohimbine, an α_2-adrenergic blocker, provokes panic-like symptoms in patients with a history of panic disorder but not in healthy control subjects (Charney et al. 1987). The serotonin system may be involved in anxiety symptoms as well; m-chlorophenylpiperazine, a serotonin agonist, increases anxiety in patients with obsessive-compulsive disorder whereas clonidine, an α_2-adrenergic agonist decreases anxiety in the same patients (Hollander et al. 1988). It is also likely that the GABA neurotransmitter system is involved in the modulation of anxiety because benzodiazepine receptors have been identified in the central nervous system which act synergistically with inhibitory GABA receptors, and it has been found that β-carboline, which blocks benzodiazepine receptors, produces anxiety in animals (Skolnick and Paul 1982). However, studies of these biologic systems must be conducted in patients with milder forms of anxiety to validate this dimension of personality psychopathology.

CONCLUSION

The study of biologic markers in personality disorders is in its early stages. More work must be done to correlate physiological findings with dimensions of personality pathology. There are many other dimensions that have not been discussed but that may be biologically mediated (e.g., sensation seeking behavior).

One area for future study is the involvement of other neurotransmitter systems in personality psychopathology other than the ones discussed in this chapter. One example is the cholinergic system. Although cholinergic functioning has been studied in affective disorders and shown to be involved in mood shifts in bipolar and depressed patients, there have been no studies to date of cholinergic functioning in affectively labile borderline patients. The GABA-benzodiazepine system needs to be investigated not only for its involvement in Axis I anxiety disorders but also for its role in anxiety-related traits. The endogenous opiate system may be found to be related to anxiety and somatization traits. This is only a partial list of biologic systems that may be involved in the development of personality disorders.

Further study is required regarding the interaction between different subtypes of receptors and presynaptic and postsynaptic receptors in the mediation of personality traits. In the past few years it has become evident that there are multiple receptors for serotonin (1A, 1B, 2) and that these subreceptor systems may mediate behavioral inhibition in both independent and reciprocal fashions (Coccaro and Murphy 1990). In addition, little is known about the interaction of various transmitter systems in the production of personality traits. For example, the serotonin system has been shown to be involved in the inhibition of aggressive behavior. However, the noradrenergic system also plays a role in aggressive acting-out behavior because blockage of β-adrenergic transmission with medications such as propranolol and pindolol have been reported to decrease aggressive behavior in schizophrenic and brain-damaged individuals (Wickham and Reed 1987; Yudofsky et al. 1981; Sorgi et al. 1986). It may be that rather than being regulated by any single transmitter system, aggressivity is mediated by a balance between the noradrenergic and serotonergic systems, with relative hypofunctioning of serotonin neurotransmission and hypersensitivity of the adrenergic system leading to aggressive and irritable personality traits. This type of interaction of neurotransmitter systems is likely to take place because it has been demonstrated in nonpsychiatric disorders (e.g., abnormalities in dopaminergic-cholinergic balance in Parkinson's disease) and hypothesized in certain Axis I disorders (e.g., abnormalities in noradrenergic-cholinergic balance in major affective disorders) (Janowsky et al. 1972).

Future studies need to address the degree of interaction between various dimensions of personality psychopathology. For example, an individual with problems in both the impulsivity and affective dimensions may exhibit dramatic episodes of behavioral dyscontrol and self-destructive behavior in response to sudden affective changes in response to real or perceived rejection as is common in many patients with borderline personality disorder. On the other hand, difficulties in the impulsivity and anxiety spectra may lead to more covert forms of self-destructive behavior (e.g., alcohol abuse and gambling).

It must be determined whether and in what manner the results of various biologic marker studies on personality disorders converge with other markers of psychiatric illness (e.g., family studies, genetic studies, treatment response). For example, studies have suggested a familial aggregation of schizotypal personality disorder and schizophrenia (Baron et al. 1985; Kendler et al. 1981). These findings are consistent with the results of psychophysiologic and dopamine studies discussed earlier that suggested similar deficits in neuro-integrative functioning and dopamine metabolism in both schizophrenia and schizotypal personality. These convergent findings suggest that it may be possible to identify a common genotype among the schizophrenia-related disorders that differ in phenotypic expression across a continuum of disorders ranging from schizophrenia to schizotypal personality disorder. Family studies have suggested a link between borderline personality and affective disorders (Soloff and Millward 1983), but in this case the studies of biologic markers have been inconclusive so that hypothesizing a genetic component to this spectrum remains premature. Treatment studies can also be correlated with the results of biologic marker studies. For example, low dose neuroleptic treatment has been found to be beneficial in schizotypal personality (Hymowitz et al. 1986), consistent with the finding of abnormal dopaminergic functioning in this population. Impulsive aggressive behavior, possibly mediated through the serotonergic system, has been found to respond to treatment with lithium (Sheard et al. 1976) with putative serotonergic properties. Further studies must be conducted to determine whether more specific serotonergic agents (e.g., fluoxetine) would be of benefit in the treatment of irritable aggressive behavior.

It would be foolish for investigators in the field of personality disorders to ignore the interaction between biologic predispositions and environment in the development of personality pathology. The way in which a particular physiological abnormality manifests itself can be markedly mediated by the interaction of the developing child and those in his or her environment: family, peers, teachers, and entertainers. For example, an affectively unstable child responding dramatically to seemingly trivial criticism may be blamed for not having more control over his or her emotions. Such a child will have difficulty developing adequate coping skills to help regulate the inevitable shifts in affect and will likely develop maladaptive coping mechanisms (e.g., acting out to relieve affective tension or obtain a helping response from others). In addition, the child will have difficulty developing an adequate internal representation of self because he or she is receiving messages from significant others (that the affective states are willful) that contradict his or her own self-assessment. The combination of these innate and learned responses might then lead to the development of borderline personality. Similar hypotheses can be generated regarding the interaction of other biologically predisposed dimensions and other putative innate characteristics, such as intelligence and motor skills, with environmental influences.

Finally, a basic question remains: does personality psychopathology occur as categorical diagnoses on a continuum with more severe psychopathology (e.g., Axis I disorders) or on a spectrum with normal personality traits? To study whether personality psychopathology occurs on a continuum with more severe psychopathology, it will be necessary to study biologic markers in individuals with varying degrees of similar psychopathology (e.g., lactate infusions and yohimbine challenges in patients with avoidant personality disorder and cholinergic challenges in borderline patients) and determine whether the degree of abnormality on a particular test correlates with the degree of psychopathology. Biologic marker studies also need to be conducted on family members of probands with personality disorders to determine the extent to which physiological abnormalities are genetically determined. Finally, further studies need to be conducted on the biologic determinants of temperment in healthy nonpersonality disordered individuals (e.g., acetylator status has been correlated with measures of hypochondriasis on the MMPI) (Saiz-Ruiz and Aguilera 1985).

Aside from the heuristic interest inherent in understanding the basis of personality development, it should be clear from the above discussion that the investigation of biologic markers in personality disorders has implications for many aspects of the clinical practice of psychiatry. Finer delineation of biologic underpinnings of personality will lead to improved nosologic systems and methods of diagnosis. Convergence of biologic and genetic data will allow for identification of individuals at risk for psychopathology. Finally, a better understanding of the biology of these disorders will lead to the development of more pharmacologically specific somatic treatments and improved psychotherapeutic techniques that can be modified based on an individual's innate temperment.

REFERENCES

Akiskal H: Subaffective disorders: dysthymic, cyclothymic, and bipolar disorders in the borderline realm. Psychiatric Clin North Am 4:25–46, 1981

American Psychiatric Association: Diagnostic and Statistical Manual of Mental Disorders, 3rd Edition. Washington, DC, American Psychiatric Association, 1980

American Psychiatric Association: Diagnostic and Statistical Manual of Mental Disorders, 3rd Edition, Revised. Washington, DC, American Psychiatric Association, 1987

Baron M, Gruen R, Asnis L, et al: Familial transmission of schizotypal and borderline personality disorders. Am J Psychiatry 142:927–934, 1985

Beeber AR, Kline MD, Pies RW, et al: Dexamethasone suppression test in hospitalized depressed patients with borderline personality disorder. J Nerv Ment Dis 5:301–303, 1984

Bell J, Lycaki H, Jones D, et al: Effect of pre-existing borderline personality disorder on clinical and EEG sleep correlates of depression. Psychiatry Res 9:115–123, 1983

Braff DL: Impaired speed of information processing in nonmedicated schizotypal patients. Schizophr Bull 7:499–508, 1981

Brown GL, Ebert MH, Goyer PF, et al: Aggression, suicide and serotonin relationships to CSF amine metabolites. Am J Psychiatry 139:741–745, 1982

Carroll BJ, Feinberg M, Greden JF, et al: A specific laboratory test for the diagnosis of melancholia: standardization, validation, and clinical utility. Arch Gen Psychiatry 38:15–22, 1981

Charney DS, Woods SW, Goodman WK, et al: Neurobiological mechanisms of panic anxiety: biochemical and behavioral correlates of yohimbine-induced panic attacks. Am J Psychiatry 144:1030–1036, 1987

Coccaro EF: Central serotonin and impulsive aggression. Br J Psychiatry (in press)

Coccaro EF, Murphy DL: Clinical significance of central serotonergic system dysfunction in major psychiatric disorders, in Serotonin in Major Psychiatric Disorders. Edited by Coccaro EF, Murphy DL. Washington, DC, American Psychiatric Press, 1990, pp 253–258

Coccaro EF, Siever LJ, Klar HM, et al: Serotonergic studies in patients with affective and personality disorders correlates with suicidal and impulsive aggressive behavior. Arch Gen Psychiatry 46:587–599, 1989

Cowley DS, Dager SR, Foster SI, et al: Clinical characteristics and response to sodium lactate in patients with infrequent panic attacks. Am J Psychiatry 144:795–798, 1987

Davidson M, Davis KL: A comparison of plasma HVA concentrations in schizophrenic patients and normal controls. Arch Gen Psychiatry 45:561–563, 1988

Davila R, Manero E, Zumarraga M, et al: Plasma HVA as a predictor of response to neuroleptic. Arch Gen Psychiatry 45:564–567, 1988

Frances A: Categorical and dimensional systems of personality diagnosis: a comparison. Compr Psychiatry 23:516–527, 1982

Garbutt JC, Loosen PT, Tipermas A, et al: The TRH test in patients with borderline personality disorder. Psychiatry Res 9:107–113, 1983

Hollander E, Fay M, Cohen B, et al: Serotonin and norepinephrine sensitivity in obsessive compulsive disorder. Paper presented at the annual meeting of the American Psychiatric Association, Montreal, Canada, May 1988

Holzman PS, Proctor LR, Levy DL, et al: Eye tracking dysfunctions in schizophrenic patients and their relatives. Arch Gen Psychiatry 31:143–151, 1974

Hymowitz P, Frances A, Jacobsberg LB, et al: Neuroleptic treatment of schizotypal personality disorders. Compr Psychiatry 27:267–271, 1986

Janowsky DS, El-Yousef MK, Davis JM, et al: A cholinergic adrenergic hypothesis of mania and depression. Lancet 2:632–635, 1972

Janowsky DS, Risch SC, Judd LL, et al: Cholinergic supersensitivity in affective disorder patients. Psychopharmacol Bull 17:129–132, 1981

Kavoussi RJ, Siever LJ, Bernstein D, et al: Plasma HVA in schizotypal personality disorder. Paper presented at the annual meeting of the American Psychiatric Association, San Francisco, CA, May 1989a

Kavoussi RJ, Siever LJ, Coccaro EF, et al: Structured interviews for borderline personality disorder. Paper presented at the annual meeting of the American Psychiatric Association, San Francisco, CA, May 1989b

Kendler KS, Gruenberg AM, Strauss JS: An independent analysis of the Copenhagen sample of the Danish adoption study of schizophrenia, II: the relationship between schizotypal personality disorder and schizophrenia. Arch Gen Psychiatry 38:982–984, 1981

Krishman KR, Davidson JR, Rayasan K, et al: The dexamethasone suppression test in borderline personality disorder. Biol Psychiatry 19:1149–1153, 1984

Langer SZ, Javoy-Agid F, Raisman R, et al: Distribution of specific high-affinity binding sites for [^{3}H] imipramine in human brain. J Neurochem 37:267–271, 1981

Lucas PB, Gardner DL, Wolkowitz OM, et al: Dysphoria associated with methylphenidate infusion in borderline personality disorder. Am J Psychiatry 144:1577–1579, 1987

Mann JJ, Stanley M, McBride PA, et al: Increased serotonin-2 and beta-adrenergic receptor binding in the frontal cortices of suicide victims. Arch Gen Psychiatry 43:954–959, 1986

McNamara E, Reynolds C, Soloff P, et al: EEG sleep evaluation of depression in borderline patients. Am J Psychiatry 141:182–186, 1984

Merritt RD, Balogh DW: The use of a backward masking paradigm to assess information processing deficits among schizotypics. J Nerv Ment Dis 172:216–224, 1984

Nuechterlein KH, Edell WS, Norris M, et al: Attentional vulnerability indicators, thought disorder, and negative symptoms. Schizophr Bull 12:408–426, 1986

Nuechterlein KH: Signal detection during vigilance and span of apprehension in non-psychotic schizotypal individuals, in Controversies in Schizophrenia. Edited by Alpert M. New York, Guilford, 1987

Nurnberger J, Berrettini W, Mendlson W, et al: Measuring cholinergic sensitivity, I: arecoline effects in bipolar patients. Biol Psychiatry 25:610–617, 1989

Pfohl B, Coryell W, Zimmerman M, et al: DSM-III personality disorders: diagnostic overlap and internal consistency of individual DSM-III criteria. Compr Psychiatry 27:21–34, 1986

Robins E, Guze SB: Establishment of diagnostic validity in psychiatric illness: its application to schizophrenia. Am J Psychiatry 126:983–987, 1970

Roy A, Adinoff B, Linnoila M: Acting out hostility in normal volunteers: negative correlations with levels of 5HIAA in cerebrospinal fluid. Psychiatry Res 24:187–194, 1988

Saiz-Ruiz J, Aguilera JC: Personality traits and acetylator status. Biol Psychiatry 20:1136–1138, 1985

Schulz SC, Cornelius J, Schulz PM, et al: The amphetamine challenge test in patients with borderline personality disorder. Am J Psychiatry 145:809–814, 1988

Sheard MH, Marini JL, Bridges CI: The effect of lithium on impulsive aggressive behavior in man. Am J Psychiatry 133:1409–1413, 1976

Siever LJ: Biological markers in schizotypal personality disorder. Schizophr Bull 11:564–574, 1985

Siever LJ, Coursey RD, Alterman IS, et al: Smooth pursuit eye movement impairment: a vulnerability marker for schizotypal personality disorder in a volunteer population. Am J Psychiatry 141:1560–1565, 1984

Siever LJ, Klar H, Coccaro E: Psychobiologic substrates of personality, in Biologic Response Styles: Clinical Implications. Edited by Klar H, Siever LJ. Washington, DC, American Psychiatric Press, 1985

Skolnick P, Paul SM: Benzodiazepine receptors in the central nervous system. Int Rev Neurobiol 23:103–140, 1982

Soloff PH, Millward JW: Psychiatric disorders in the families of borderline patients. Arch Gen Psychiatry 40:37–44, 1983

Soloff PH, George A, Nathan RS: The dexamethasone suppression test in patients with borderline personality disorder. Am J Psychiatry 139:1621–1623, 1982

Sorgi PJ, Ratey JJ, Polakoff S: Beta-adrenergic blockers for the control of aggressive behaviors in patients with chronic schizophrenia. Am J Psychiatry 143:775–776, 1986

Stanley M, Viggilio J, Gershon S: Tritiated imipramine binding sites are decreased in the frontal cortex of suicides. Science 216:1337–1339, 1982

Steele TS: Depression, borderline disorder, and the DST. Am J Psychiatry 140:818–820, 1983

Sternbach H, Fleming J, Extein I: The dexamethasone suppression and thyrotropin releasing hormone tests in depressed borderline patients. Psychoneuroendocrinology 8:459–462, 1983

Valzelli L: Psychobiology of Aggression and Violence. New York, Raven, 1981

Virkkunen M, Nuutila A, Goodwin FK, et al: Cerebrospinal fluid metabolite levels in male arsonists. Arch Gen Psychiatry 44:241–247, 1987

Wickham EA, Reed JV: Lithium for the control of aggressive and self-mutilating behavior. Int J Clin Psychopharmacol 2:181–190, 1987

Widiger TA, Trull TJ, Hurt SW, et al: A multidimensional scaling of the DSM-III personality disorders. Arch Gen Psychiatry 44:557–563, 1987

Widiger TA, Frances A, Spitzer RL, et al: The DSM-III-R personality disorders: an overview. Am J Psychiatry 145:786–795, 1988

Yudofsky S, Williams D, Gorman J: Propranolol in the treatment of rage and violent behavior in patients with chronic brain syndromes. Am J Psychiatry 138:218–220, 1981

Chapter 5

Pharmacotherapy and Borderline Subtypes

Paul H. Soloff, M.D.
Anselm George, M.D.
Jack Cornelius, M.D.
Swami Nathan, M.D.
Patricia Schulz, M.S.W.

Chapter 5

Pharmacotherapy and Borderline Subtypes

The creation of a borderline personality disorder (BPD) was the inevitable result of early efforts to define clear boundaries between neurotic and psychotic diagnoses or levels of functioning. After nearly a century of wrestling with the concept, the validity of the borderline as a discrete diagnostic entity remains controversial and unsettling.

Early empirical writers defined borderline as a subschizophrenic disorder emphasizing the patients' vulnerability to the psychotic thought process. Patients diagnosed as latent, ambulatory, or pseudoneurotic schizophrenic were described as odd, eccentric characters with mild disorders of thinking, intense ambivalence, and transient loss of reality testing under stress. They occupied the diagnostic border with schizophrenia and the psychotic adaptational level. Many BPD patients demonstrated not only a vulnerability to loss of control of thinking, but also of affect and behavior. These were prominent features of patients whose baseline behavior was more affective, labile, and impulsive. A spectrum concept of borderline extended the definition to include dramatic, impulsive, hysteroid patients who also demonstrated transient loss of reality testing under stress. The core pathology of the emotionally unstable hysteroid group was affective dysregulation and impulsivity, manifested in anger, depression, and impulsive and self-destructive behaviors. Loss of reality testing in this group seemed secondary to affective turmoil and was more consistent with mood-congruent distortions of cognition and perception seen in patients with pure affective disorder. With a change in diagnostic fashion, the borderline concept shifted from a subschizophrenic to a subaffective disorder (Stone 1979). The redefinition is so complete that DSM-III (American Psychiatric Association 1980) now reserves the term *borderline* exclusively for the unstable affective variant,

This work is supported by NIMH Grants MH-35392, MH-00658, and CRC MH-30915.

relegating the historical schizotypal features to a separate schizotypal personality disorder (SPD). However, empirical studies continue to demonstrate extensive overlap of these two symptom dimensions among patients clinically diagnosed as borderline (George and Soloff 1986).

The heterogeneity of this disorder poses significant methodological problems to any systematic effort at treatment. The borderline patient presents with various affective, schizotypal, and impulsive behavioral symptoms, often with differing patterns in the same patient over time. Efforts to resolve this heterogeneity and define the relationship of borderline to affective or schizophrenic spectrum disorders have included family and twin studies (Akiskal 1981; Andrulonis et al. 1981; Baron et al. 1985; Loranger et al. 1982; Pope et al. 1983; Schulz et al. 1986, in press; Soloff and Millward 1983; Stone 1981; Torgerson 1984), neuroendocrine (Garbutt et al. 1983; Nathan et al. 1986; Sternbach 1983) and sleep studies (Bell et al. 1983; Reynolds et al. 1985), long-term follow-up studies (McGlashan 1986; Plakun et al. 1985), and pharmacological challenge strategies (Kellner et al. 1987; Lucas et al. 1987; Schulz et al. 1987). Taken together, these studies suggest a relationship for DSM-III BPD to the affective disorders spectrum, although as a discrete entity in its own right.

The category of SPD has stirred controversy because of the mix of state and trait symptoms used as diagnostic criteria (Frances 1985; Kendler 1985). State symptoms, such as mild paranoid ideation or referential thinking, illusions, and perceptual distortions are prominently found among DSM-III BPD patients as transient responses to stress. Trait symptoms such as odd eccentric behavior, absence of close friends, and constricted affect are related more to the negative symptoms of the schizophrenia spectrum. The genetic link to schizophrenia has been demonstrated for patients with "borderline schizophrenia," a clinical definition that is the progenitor of DSM-III SPD, but not for patients meeting criteria for both BPD and SPD, the so-called "mixed" borderline group (schizotypal borderline) (Baron et al. 1985; Gunderson et al. 1983; Kendler et al. 1981; Torgerson 1984). This confusion appears to be a product of the artificial definitions of DSM. The schizotypal symptoms of patients with BPD appear to be the acute positive state symptoms, whereas schizotypal patients with familial schizophrenia are characterized by negative trait symptoms. Depending on the source of patients and study methods, up to half of DSM-III criteria-defined borderline patients may meet criteria for SPD (Spitzer 1979; Spitzer et al. 1979).

We selected the method of pharmacological behavioral dissection to attempt further characterization of BPD into meaningful clinical subtypes. Pharmacological characterization of BPD is an appealing research strategy as it defines empirical indications for medication use through analysis of main effects and simultaneously can provide data for the definition of clinical subtypes through medication response. Methodological problems in this approach include the extensive comorbidity of borderline with Axis I disorders, especially major depression, as well as difficulty delineating borderline from its syndromal close neighbors dysthymic, cyclothymic, and bipolar II disorders, and the confusion of state and trait symptom variables.

With an empirical theoretical approach, we conducted the first double-blind placebo controlled comparison of antidepressant and neuroleptic medication in criteria-defined borderline inpatients defined by Gunderson's Diagnostic Interview for Borderlines, which surveys micropsychotic and affective pathology (Gunderson et al. 1981). After clinical prejudice and practice, we assumed the antidepressant would be most effective in unstable affective BPD patients and the neuroleptic in schizotypal-mixed borderline (SPD/BPD, SPD) patients. We hoped that medication response patterns would provide an empirical validation for the separation of the two subtypes.

METHODS

This study was conducted among consecutive inpatients at the Western Psychiatric Institute and Clinic, a University of Pittsburgh affiliated hospital. Patients were referred for study evaluation if their primary clinician made a presumptive clinical diagnosis of BDP, SPD, or SPD/BPD. A cutoff score of ≥7.0 was required on Gunderson's Diagnostic Interview for Borderlines (Gunderson et al. 1981). A DSM-III subtype diagnosis of BPD, SPD, or SPD/BPD was made on the basis of direct patient interviews. Exclusion criteria were defined for chronicity, medical disorder, and organicity. Patients were excluded from the study if they warranted a current Research Diagnostic Criteria (RDC) diagnosis of schizophrenia, schizoaffective disorder, manic disorder, bipolar disorder with mania, or hypomania by clinical evaluation or interview on the Schedule for Affective Disorders and Schizophrenia (SADS), or a valid past diagnosis by history, chart review, or interview on the SADS-Lifetime Version. Patients meeting RDC by clinical history or SADS for a current diagnosis of major depression were included but coded for separate statistical analysis.

After a minimum of 7 days without medication, patients were required to demonstrate sufficient continuing symptom severity to warrant pharmacotherapy on the Global Assessment Scale (GAS < 50), and either the Hamilton Rating Scale for Depression, 24-item format (HRS-24 ≥ 17), or the Inpatient Multidimensional Psychiatric Rating Scale (IMPS ≥ 66). With these methods, 90 inpatients were recruited from among consecutive acute admissions and randomly assigned to receive haloperidol (up to 12 mg/day), amitriptyline (up to 150 mg/day), or placebo (6 tablets/day) in addition to the usual group, milieu, or individual therapies available on the inpatient unit. If necessary the medication dose was reduced for patient comfort and, on rare occasion, increased to enhance clinical effect. Early experience prompted a decrease in the maximal haloperidol dose to 6 mg (1-mg tablets), which was thought to be sufficient to produce change and minimize side effects. Plasma was obtained weekly for analysis of haloperidol and amitriptyline plus nortriptyline metabolites, allowing retrospective control over adequacy of treatment.

The pharmacotherapy trial lasted 5 weeks with weekly self and observer ratings of global functioning (GAS and Symptom Checklist 90 [SCL-90]), depression (HRS-24 and Beck Depression Inventory [BDI]), psychoticism (IMPS and Schizotypal Symptom Inventory [SSI]), hostility (Buss-Durkee Hostility Inventory [BDHI]), impulsive behavior (Ward Scale of Impulse Action Patterns), and impulsive traits (Barratt Impulsiveness Scale [BIS] and Self-Report Test of Impulse Control [STIC]).

A minimum of 2 weeks receiving medication was required to include data for end-point analysis. Patients who left the hospital after this point were allowed to complete the protocol as outpatients.

Statistical tests were performed by paired t tests for changes within each group and by analysis of covariance for differences between groups, using week 1 (baseline) as the covariate and the average of weeks 5 and 6 as outcome. (All tests are two-tailed.) An average of weeks 5 and 6 was used to compensate for any bias introduced by the pending hospital discharge of patients at the end of protocol. For this analysis, we present medication effects specific to each DSM-III diagnostic subtype and results of a two-way interaction analysis between diagnosis and medication. The entire sample analysis is presented in detail elsewhere (Soloff et al. 1989).

RESULTS

Among the 85 patients completing the minimum medication trial for inclusion in end-point analysis, approximately 25.9% were male and 74.1% female. The mean age of the study sample was 25.1 years. Diagnostically, there were 34 patients with DSM-III BPD (38.9%) and 51 with either DSM-III SPD (4.4%) or SPD/BPD (56.7%).

Patients with SPD/BPD and SPD alone were pooled to allow a comparison of Diagnostic Interview for Borderlines (DIB)-defined borderline patients with and without schizotypy. (We refer to the schizotypal group as *schizotypal mixed*.) Mean number of schizotypal diagnostic criteria (DSM-III) for the entire study sample was 3.95 items with a median of 3.93. The mean number of DSM-III BPD criteria was 6.71 for the overall sample (median 6.89).

Patients with pure BPD were characterized at baseline by a greater number of DSM-III BPD criteria compared with the schizotypal-mixed group (7.0 vs. 6.5, $t = 1.96$, $P = .053$). Compared with the schizotypal-mixed borderline group, patients with pure BPD had higher statement scores on the DIB in the categories of special achievements and active social life resulting in a higher overall Social Adaptation Section Score. These items attest to adequacy of social functioning (Table 5-1). By definition, schizotypal-mixed patients had more schizotypal diagnostic criteria (4.9 vs. 2.4, $t = 12.45$, $P < .0005$). On the DIB, this was manifested by higher scores on the items assessing derealization, depersonalization, paranoid experience, transitory hallucinations or delusions, social isolation, elation, flat affect, or hypomanic behavior. This is summarized in the Psychosis Section Score. At baseline, the overall sample was moderately symptomatic, with a mean GAS of 42.2, an HRS (17 items) of 17.6, a BDI of 31.8, and an IMPS of 121.0. Patients with the schizotypal-mixed borderline disorder were more severely symptomatic at baseline than pure BPD patients (Table 5-1). They had significantly lower mean baseline scores on global functioning (GAS), higher mean scores on general severity index (SCL-90), depression (HRS-17 and HRS-24), and schizotypal symptoms (SSI: positive symptom total, SSI: sum total, and IMPS total score). The schizotypal-mixed group was significantly more impaired at baseline than the BPD group on 6 of 10 SCL-90 subscales (somatization, obsessive compulsive, anxiety, hostility, phobic anxiety, psychoticism). Note that the two groups did not differ on measures of anger, hostility, or impulsiveness—key diagnostic criteria for BPD.

PHARMACOTHERAPY RESULTS

Overall Sample

Pharmacotherapy results by subtype must be viewed in the context of the overall sample response comparing the three medication conditions. After a brief summary of overall sample responsiveness, specific effects of medications will be presented within diagnostic subtypes. (Results of the pharmacotherapy trial in the overall sample are

Table 5-1. Pretreatment comparisons of DIB-defined borderline patients by DSM-III subtype

	Mean BPD alone ($n = 34$)	Mean SPD/BPD and SPD alone ($n = 51$)	Paired t tests and P
Diagnostic variables			
DSM-III BPD criteria	7.0	6.5	1.96*
DSM-III SPD criteria	2.4	4.9	−12.45****
DIB statement scores			
Special achievements	1.15	0.71	2.32**
Active social life	1.03	0.59	2.55**
Social adaptation section score	5.12	4.20	2.63**
Elated, flat, hypomanic	0.12	0.13	−2.06**
Derealization	0.53	1.31	−3.42****
Depersonalization	0.79	1.13	−2.05**
Paranoid experience	0.74	1.45	−4.27****
Hallucinations/delusions	0.09	0.49	−3.51****
Socially isolated	0.09	0.61	−4.76****
Psychosis section score	3.97	6.88	−4.15****
Dependent variables (baseline)			
Global assessment scale	43.9	41.0	2.61***
SCL-90: general severity	1.55	1.94	−2.75***
Hamilton Rating Scale-17 items	16.4	18.4	−2.03**
Hamilton Rating Scale-24 items	23.0	26.6	−2.57***
Schizotypal symptom inventory (Pos. Sxs.)	5.89	8.97	−4.95****
Schizotypal symptom inventory (Sum)	11.14	18.00	−4.66****
IMPS: paranoid	2.44	5.11	−2.27**
IMPS: perceptual distortions	2.32	5.23	−3.12***
IMPS: retardation	4.00	6.73	−2.11**
IMPS: total score	112.3	126.8	−1.94**
SCL-90: somatization	0.89	1.39	−3.11***
SCL-90: obsessive compulsive	1.63	2.25	−3.44****
SCL-90: anxiety	1.66	2.07	−1.96*
SCL-90: hostility	1.41	1.96	−2.48***
SCL-90: phobia	0.88	1.50	−3.03**
SCL-90: psychoticism	1.18	1.56	−2.20**

Note. BPD = borderline personality; SPD = schizotypal personality disorder; DIB = diagnostic interview for borderline; IMPS = inpatient multidimensional psychiatric rating scale.
*$P \leq .1$. **$P \leq .05$. ***$P \leq .01$. ****$P \leq .001$.

presented in detail elsewhere [Soloff et al. 1989].) In the overall sample, haloperidol produced significant improvement compared with placebo in all symptom areas including global functioning, depression, hostility, schizotypal symptoms, and impulsive behavior. More specifically, haloperidol was superior to placebo on the GAS, HRS (24 items), BDI, BDHI (indirect hostility), SSI, IMPS total score, and the Ward Scale of Impulse Action Patterns. In addition, haloperidol was superior to placebo on 6 of 10 SCL-90 self-rated factors including depression, obsessive compulsive, interpersonal sensitivity, hostility, paranoid ideation, and psychoticism. In contrast, the significant effects of amitriptyline versus placebo were limited to measures of depression, specifically the HRS (24 items) and BDI. There was no relationship between a diagnosis of major depression on Axis I and responsiveness to amitriptyline. Indeed, amitriptyline nonresponders fared significantly worse than placebo nonresponders and demonstrated increases in suicidality, referential thinking, and assaultiveness (Soloff et al. 1986). (The independence of major depression and antidepressant responsiveness in BPD patients was recently confirmed by Cowdry [1988] using tranycypromine in DIB-defined BPD outpatients.)

Medication Response by Subtype

Analysis of covariance for the three medication conditions was repeated for each subtype (Table 5-2). Among patients with pure BPD, five outcome measures reflected significant effects of medication: depression (BDI), hostility (BDHI: indirect hostility, negativism; SCL-90: hostility), and perceived impulsive control (STIC). Medication effects were suggested but not significant in global function (GAS) and in the number and severity of schizotypal symptoms. Drug versus placebo comparisons were calculated for these significant or near significant variables. The greatest response to haloperidol was found in the areas of global functioning, schizotypal symptoms, hostility, and impulse control. Effects on subjective depression did not achieve statistical significance. The response to amitriptyline among pure unstable BPD patients was strongest in selected measures of hostility and impulse control with a near significant effect on subjective depression (BDI). Thus, in affectively unstable BPD patients, a modest antidepressant effect was attributable to amitriptyline, subjective control of hostility and impulsivity to both drugs and relief of schizotypal symptoms, and overall severity to haloperidol.

In the schizotypal-mixed borderline sample, the overall comparison of drugs and placebo yielded significant medication effects in depres-

Table 5-2. Response to medication within DSM-III subtypes

Outcome measure	BPD (N = 34)		
	AMI vs. HAL vs. PLC (F,P)	HAL (n = 11) vs. PLC (n = 12) (F,P)	AMI (n = 11) vs. PLC (n = 12) (F,P)
Beck Depression Inventory	4.99, <.05	NS	3.26*
Buss-Durkee: indirect hostility	3.44, <.05	3.42, <.1	6.29**
Buss-Durkee: negativism	6.88, <.01	NS	9.41***
Self-report test of impulse control (moral)	4.28, <.05	6.68, <.05	5.93**
SCL-90: hostility	3.50, <.05	6.46, <.05	NS
Global assessment scale	2.85, <.1	6.45, <.05	NS
Schizotypal symptom inventory (Pos. Sxs.)	2.76, <.1	4.67, <.05	NS
Schizotypal symptom inventory (Sum)	3.21, <.1	5.64, <.05	NS

Table 5-2. Response to medication within DSM-III subtypes *(continued)*

	SPD/BPD and SPD (N = 51)		
Outcome measure	AMI vs. HAL vs. PLC (F,P)	HAL (n = 17) vs. PLC (n = 16) (F,P)	AMI (n = 18) vs. PLC (n = 16) (F,P)
Beck Depression Inventory	5.48***	7.52**	6.30**
Barratt Impulsiveness Scale (self-control)	6.50***	9.05***	10.52***
IMPS: hostile belligerance	3.68**	5.58**	NS
IMPS: paranoia	3.89**	4.03**	NS
SCL-90: obsessive compulsive	3.45**	5.46**	NS
SCL-90: interpersonal sensitivity	4.52**	5.53**	NS
SCL-90: paranoid ideation	4.21**	6.40**	NS
Buss-Durkee: suspicious	2.53	5.00**	NS
SCL-90: depression	3.05*	3.63*	NS
SCL-90: hostility	2.55*	4.05**	NS
Ward Scale of Impulse Action	2.75*	4.72**	NS

Note. BPD = borderline personality disorder; SPD = schizotypal personality disorder; IMPS = inpatient multidimensional psychiatric rating scale; AMI = amitriptyline; HAL = haloperidol; PLC = placebo.
*P ≤ .1. **P ≤ .05. ***P ≤ .01. ****P ≤ .001.

sion (BDI), interpersonal sensitivity and obsessive-compulsive factors (SCL-90), hostility (IMPS), paranoid ideation (IMPS and SCL-90), and a measure of trait impulsivity (BIS). Trends toward significance were found in related scales: depression (SCL-90), hostility (SCL-90 and BDHI), and impulsive ward behavior (Ward Scale of Impulse Action Patterns). Surprisingly, there were no significant medication effects in scales sensitive to schizotypal symptoms. Response to haloperidol was apparent on a broad spectrum of related affective measures (BDI, SCL-90, obsessive compulsive, and interpersonal sensitivity) and measures of paranoid ideation, hostility, and impulsive ward behavior. There were no significant effects of haloperidol on observed schizotypal symptoms in this borderline subtype, which is defined by the presence of such symptoms. Amitriptyline efficacy in the schizotypal-mixed subtype was noted in subjective depression (BDI), with some enhanced perception of self-control over impulsiveness (BIS).

Thus, in schizotypal-mixed patients, antidepressant efficacy is shared equally by both drugs; haloperidol appears to be a broad spectrum treatment for hostility, paranoid ideation, actual impulsive ward behavior, and the broad affective spectrum (interpersonal sensitivity and obsessive compulsive).

The most critical statistical test of the effect of subtype on medication response is the medication-by-diagnosis interaction analysis. No statistically significant interaction between medication and subtype diagnosis was found on any outcome measure.

DISCUSSION

As a contribution to the validation of borderline subtypes, ours is largely a negative report. We were unable to demonstrate a clear pharmacological behavioral dissection using medication responsiveness to separate diagnostic subtypes. The failure to demonstrate significant interaction between subtype diagnosis and medication response appears to be due to the broad spectrum effectiveness of haloperidol, the significant effect of neuroleptic agents on overall symptom severity (independent of specific content), and the relatively modest magnitude of change. It is not surprising that the more severely impaired schizotypal-mixed patients show the clearest response to haloperidol. Rather than being a discrete subtype, the schizotypal-mixed variant may well represent a dimension of severity. These data suggest that haloperidol is a useful treatment against symptom severity across the entire borderline spectrum and that the more severe or schizotypal the disorder, the more strongly a neuroleptic agent is indicated.

Symptoms not demonstrating significant medication effects showed either strong placebo responses (e.g., schizotypal symptoms) or modest but equal change across all three conditions (e.g., HRS). An additional cause of our failure at pharmacological dissection was the poor performance of amitriptyline. This drug may be an unfortunate choice of antidepressant in a syndrome manifested primarily by atypical affective features. Studies using monoamine oxidase inhibitor antidepressants may prove more effective.

Our results challenge the simple clinical prejudice of prescribing neuroleptic agents solely for the schizotypal features and antidepressants for the affective features of BPD patients. Indeed, the paradoxical worsening among amitriptyline nonresponders suggests danger in the blanket prescription of antidepressants for BPD patients who also meet DSM criteria for major depression.

Finally, the failure of pharmacological dissection may be due to difficulty in separating subtypes by DSM syndrome definitions, i.e., separating pure BPD from schizotypal-mixed patients using a polythetic menu method. George and Soloff (1986) have shown at least one and an average of six schizotypal symptoms in patients defined as pure DSM-III BPD. DSM-III definition of subtypes allows for such heterogeneity as to render a pharmacological dissection most difficult. Large medication effects or extensive sample sizes would be required to overcome such bias. The mixed BPD patient represents a challenge to the validity of the DSM definition, i.e., Does the mixed SPD/BPD patient have one disorder or two?

Future analyses will focus on medication effects to identify predictors of response by symptom cluster (i.e., independent of DSM subtype). We hope that these studies will help to define a more specific pharmacotherapy of BPDs.

REFERENCES

Akiskal H: Subaffective disorders: dysthymia, cyclothymic and bipolar II disorders in the borderline realm. Psychiatr Clin North Am 4:25–46, 1981

American Psychiatric Association: Diagnostic and Statistical Manual of Mental Disorders, 3rd Edition. Washington, DC, American Psychiatric Association, 1980

Andrulonis P, Glueck B, Stroebel C: Organic brain dysfunction and the borderline syndrome. Psychiatr Clin North Am 4:47–66, 1981

Baron M, Gruen R, Asnis L, et al: Familial transmission of schizotypal and borderline personality disorders. Am J Psychiatry 142:927–933, 1985

Bell J, Lycaki H, Jones O, et al: Effect of pre-existing borderline personality disorder on clinical and EEG sleep correlates of depression. Psychiatry Res 9:115–123, 1983

Cowdry R, Gardner D: Pharmacotherapy of borderline personality disorder: alprazolam, carbamazepine, trifluoperazine and tranylcypromine. Arch Gen Psychiatry 45:111–119, 1988

Frances A: Validating schizotypal personality disorders: problems with the schizophrenia connection. Schizophr Bull 11:595–598, 1985

Garbutt JC, Loosen PT, Tipermas A, et al: The TRH test in patients with borderline personality disorder. Psychiatry Res 9:107–113, 1983

George A, Soloff P: Schizotypal symptoms in patients with borderline personality disorders. Am J Psychiatry 143:212–215, 1986

Gunderson J, Kolb J, Austin V: The Diagnostic Interview for Borderline Patients. Am J Psychiatry 138:896–903, 1981

Gunderson J, Siever L, Spaulding E: The search for a schizotype: crossing the border again. Arch Gen Psychiatry 40:15–22, 1983

Kellner CH, Post RM, Putnam F, et al: Intravenous procaine as a probe of limbic system activity in psychiatric patients and normal controls. Biol Psychiatry 22:1107–1126, 1987

Kendler K: Diagnostic approaches to schizotypal personality disorder: a historical perspective. Schizophr Bull 11:538–553, 1985

Kendler K, Gruenberg A, Strauss J: An independent analysis of the Copenhagen sample of the Danish adoption study of schizophrenia, II: the relationship between schizotypal personality disorder and schizophrenia. Arch Gen Psychiatry 38:982–984, 1981

Loranger A, Oldham J, Tulis E: Familial transmission of borderline personality disorder. Am J Psychiatry 39:795–802, 1982

Lucas PB, Gardner DL, Wolkowitz OM, et al: Dysphoria associated with methylphenidate infusion in borderline personality disorder. Am J Psychiatry 144:1577–1579, 1987

McGlashan TA: The Chestnut Lodge follow-up study, III: long term outcome of borderline personalities. Arch Gen Psychiatry 47:20–30, 1986

Nathan RS, Soloff PH, George A, et al: DST and TRH tests in borderline personality disorder, in Biological Psychiatry, 1985. Edited by Shagass C, Josiassen RC, Bridger WH, et al. New York, Elsevier, 1986, pp 563–565

Plakun EM, Burkhardt PE, Muller JP: Fourteen year follow-up of borderline and schizotypal personality disorders. Compr Psychiatry 26:448–455, 1985

Pope HG, Jonas JM, Hudson JI, et al: The validity of DSM III borderline personality disorder. Arch Gen Psychiatry 40:23–30, 1983

Reynolds CF III, Soloff PH, Kuper DJ, et al: Depression in borderline patients: a prospective EEG sleep study. Psychiatry Res 14:1–15, 1985

Schulz PM, Schulz SC, Goldberg SC, et al: Diagnosis of the relatives of schizotypal and borderline patients. J Nerv Ment Dis 174:457–463, 1986

Schulz SC, Cornelius J, Jarret DB, et al: Pharmacodynamic probes in personality disorders. Psychopharmacol Bull 23:337–341, 1987

Schulz PM, Soloff PH, Kelly T, et al: A family history study of borderline subtypes. J Pers Disord 3:217–229, 1989

Soloff P, Millward J: Psychiatric disorders in the families of borderline patients. Arch Gen Psychiatry 40:37–44, 1983

Soloff PH, George A, Nathan RS, et al: Paradoxical effects of amitriptyline on borderline patients. Am J Psychiatry 143:1603–1605, 1986

Soloff P, George A, Nathan RS, et al: Amitriptyline vs. haloperidol in borderlines: final outcomes and predictors of response. J Clin Psychopharmacol 9:238–246, 1989

Spitzer R: Crossing the border to borderline personality and borderline schizophrenia. Arch Gen Psychiatry 36:17–24, 1979

Spitzer R, Endicott J, Gibbon M: Justification for separating schizotypal and borderline personality disorders. Schizophr Bull 5:95–104, 1979

Sternbach HA, Fleming J, Extein I, et al: The dexamethasone suppression and thyrotropin releasing hormone tests in depressed borderline patients. Psychoneuroendocrinology 8:459–462, 1983

Stone M: Contemporary shift of the borderline concept from a sub-schizophrenic to a subaffective disorder. Psychiatr Clin North Am 2:577–594, 1979

Stone M: Psychiatrically ill relatives of borderline patients: a family study. Psychiatr Q 58:71–83, 1981

Torgerson S: Genetic and nosologic aspects of schizotypal and borderline personality disorders: a twin study. Arch Gen Psychiatry 41:546–554, 1984

Chapter 6

Is Narcissistic Personality Disorder a Valid Diagnosis?

John G. Gunderson, M.D.
Elsa Ronningstam, Ph.D.

Chapter 6

Is Narcissistic Personality Disorder a Valid Diagnosis?

BACKGROUND

The question of whether narcissistic personality disorder (NPD) is a valid diagnosis is derived, in part, from the historical fact that the term *narcissistic* has been used in diverse ways (Cooper 1982; Morrison 1986; Pulver 1970). Within the psychoanalytic literature these ways have included the following: 1) a developmental process (stage or pathway) giving rise to a personality trait more or less present in everyone, 2) excessive investment of libidinal energy in the self and an inability to invest in others, and 3) a grandiose view of one's self that exceeds that which is realistic. According to these three conceptual frameworks, the clinical evidence for pathological narcissism would be found in a failure to achieve a cohesive sense of self; in preoccupation with oneself accompanied by a disregard or insensitivity to others; or in an exaggerated valuation of one's talents, achievements, uniqueness, and specialness, accompanied by a vulnerability when confronted with irrefutable realities.

At another level, various psychoanalytic contributors have given differing emphases to the characteristics they consider to be core, essential, or defining aspects of pathological narcissism. Reich (1953) emphasized identification with a grandiose ego ideal. Modell (1975) emphasized the denial of the importance of object relationships. Kohut (1971, 1977) emphasized dependence on the self-regulating functions that others serve. Morrison (1986) asserted the centrality of the need for a sense of uniqueness, and Kernberg (1975) added that projected oral rage is also a central feature.

There have been limited efforts to systematically identify the descriptive characteristics of patients with pathological narcissism. The adoption of narcissistic personality as a category in DSM-III (American Psychiatric Association 1980) was stimulated by the widespread clinical use of the term. DSM-III criteria for NPD were created from a review of the available literature by members of that committee. Like the DSM-III committee, Akhtar and Thomson (1982) also reviewed the previous literature in their effort to identify descriptive characteristics for people with NPD. Because both efforts were tied to previous literature, they partially reflected the early contributions of Kernberg (1975). He has subsequently continued to be the primary contributor in developing a descriptive characterization of such patients (1984). An analysis of these three efforts by one of us has shown a striking lack of consensus in the criterion lists that they derived (Ronningstam 1988). This finding contrasts with the impression of high concordance about the general themes (such as grandiosity, interpersonal relations marked by excessive envy or deficient empathy, and a self-esteem vulnerable to intense reactions) that the criteria sets all try to reflect.

Both the diversity of the formulations for narcissistic pathology and the discrepancies within proposed descriptive efforts underscore the questions as to whether a specific type of narcissistic pathology exists and whether it can be identified. To answer these questions, we have undertaken a series of empirical studies.

ASSESSING NARCISSISTIC TRAITS

We compared a sample of patients with a broad range of psychopathology to patients who had received clinical diagnoses of pathological narcissism. No effort was made to specifically select patients with an NPD as a primary diagnosis. Thus, this was a study of trait rather than disorder (Ronningstam and Gunderson 1988).

We began with an effort to operationalize descriptive characteristics from the previous literature into an interview. In total, the interview covered 27 descriptive characteristics and had good overall interrater reliability. We then applied this interview to a sample of 51 patients who were comprised from 36 consecutive admissions supplemented by 15 patients whose clinicians felt they had narcissistic problems. Only 5 of the patients had a primary diagnosis of NPD. Eighteen others were labeled as narcissistic but it was in conjunction with various other diagnoses. We compared these 23 patients to the 28 patients to whom no narcissistic label was assigned.

As shown in Table 6-1, 15 of 27 characteristics were significantly more common in the patients given narcissistic diagnoses. Included in those 15 characteristics were 7 of 9 criteria used in DSM-III-R (American Psychiatric Association 1987).

This study showed that many of the characteristics attributed to NPD in the literature could be reliably identified and were found with higher frequency among patients clinicians called narcissistic. This study also raised questions as to whether some characteristics attributed to pathological narcissism in the literature are specific. Thus, this study encouraged further developing a method for studying pathological narcissism and for conducting similar studies with more rigorously defined samples of narcissistic patients and different comparison groups.

DIAGNOSTIC INTERVIEW FOR NARCISSISM

In our study of a narcissistic trait, we began to develop a Diagnostic Interview for Narcissism (DIN) by operationalizing characterizations of narcissistic persons found in the previous literature. It then evolved by adding characteristics based on our clinical experience including that which resulted from the multiple exposures to narcissistic persons during the 2-year period of this instrument's development. As such, the DIN now reflects the impressions gathered during the course of systematically examining samples of narcissistic patients.

Table 6-1. Narcissistic versus nonnarcissistic patients (*t* test)

Statement[a]		Corresponding DSM-III-R criterion	*P*
ST-9	Needs attention/admiration	7	.0000
ST-14	Haughty/arrogant/boastful/ pretentious		.0000
ST-19	Reaction to criticism/defeat	1	.0000
ST-7	Self-centered/referential		.0000
ST-6	Superiority		.0001
ST-11	Devaluation/contempt		.001
ST-13	Entitlement	6	.001
ST-33	Perversions/promiscuity		.003
ST-28	High achievements		.004
ST-5	Uniqueness	4	.005
ST-3	Grandiose fantasies	5	.005
ST-15	Exploitiveness	2	.006
ST-1	Exaggeration	3	.01
ST-21	Aggressive reactions		.02
ST-10	Idealization		.04

[a]Those that were significantly more common in the narcissistic sample.

Content

The content of the interview includes 33 descriptive characteristics that are divided into five sections: grandiosity, interpersonal relations, reactiveness, affects and mood states, and social and moral adaptation (Table 6-2). These divisions are based on our conceptual organization of the 33 characteristics.

The grandiosity section begins with general questions about the patient's functional history and how he or she would describe himself or herself as a person. It then moves into specific inquiries that are directed at eliciting whether and how the person has unrealistically elevated views of himself in terms of special abilities, invulnerability, self-sufficiency, and uniqueness.

Characteristics in the interpersonal relations section are to a large extent derived from psychoanalytic psychotherapeutic literature. Issues such as the narcissistic person's tendency to idealize others and to lack empathy draw heavily on writings from Kohut (1971, 1977). Other characteristics that describe the narcissistic person's putative devaluative, contemptuous, entitled, and exploitative style are more heavily drawn from the descriptions by Kernberg (1975, 1984). Although psychotherapists primarily write about observations within psychotherapy, the interview is directed at eliciting evidence for the presence of such characteristics in the patient's usual interpersonal style with significant others.

The reactiveness section evaluates whether a person has unusually intense reactions to criticism, defeat, or disappointment. Specific inquiries directed at whether a person has felt that such experiences were motivated by envy and whether they result in feeling deep shame, humiliation, and rage highlights the narcissistic person's extreme sensitivity and his or her inappropriate exaggerated responses.

Table 6-2.   Interrater reliability (Pearson's r) on sections score and total scores ($N = 13$)

Section	Pearson's r	P
1	.87	.000
2	.82	.000
3	.85	.000
4	.96	.000
5	.98	.000
Total score	.97	.000

The affects and mood states section looks for sustained and deep feelings of emptiness, boredom, meaninglessness, and futility. Sustained feelings of inner badness was included because it is characteristic of borderline patients (Gunderson 1984; Robbins 1982) and was weighed against the narcissistic diagnosis.

The section on social and moral adaptation is based on the expectation that narcissistic people manage high achievements while maintaining superficial self-serving values and morals. A distinction is drawn between the narcissistic person who may break laws in a state of anger or for reasons of personal aggrandizement and a person who repeatedly engages in antisocial behavior (usually for monetary or other external gain). The latter pattern is considered typical of the antisocial person and was weighed against the narcissistic diagnosis.

Scoring

The statements can be added to form total section scores and a total interview score. The interview total score (a sum of all 33 statements) provides an overall index of the level of the patient's narcissistic pathology. This corresponds with the use of narcissism as a dimensional personality trait as opposed to the use of narcissism to describe a categorical diagnostic entity.

To determine whether DIN could be used to identify patients with NPD, we established cutoffs for the five total section scores. As recommended by Baldessarini et al. (1983), we set cutoffs for the section score that gave the highest sum total on tests of sensitivity, specificity, and positive and negative predictive power. These tests were conducted on a carefully selected sample of 29 patients with clinically identified NPD who were compared to 53 other psychiatric patients. Because results in the earlier trait study and results in the new samples both showed that grandiosity (section 1) and interpersonal relations (section 2) contained the most discriminating features of what is clinically judged to be pathological narcissism, these two sections were given heavier weighting. The section 1 total score was scaled to a maximum of 4 and section 2 was scaled to 3. The other three sections had maximum scaled scores of 2. Thus, the total scaled DIN score was in the range of 0–13. Using patient samples with high proportions of near-neighbor (borderline and antisocial) patients, we identified a scaled total interview cutoff of 9 or 10 to qualify for a diagnosis of NPD. The cutoff of 9 is sufficient under most circumstances and provides accurate diagnostic classification of NPD patients approximately 80% of the time. The cutoff of 10 is desirable for making more difficult differential diagnoses (as with antisocial personality disorder) or to assure maximal diagnostic certainty.

Reliability

Interrater reliabilities were calculated with the weighted kappa coefficient on all statements. Mean weighted kappas for all statements was 0.69. Adequate reliability was achieved for 29 of 33 statements. In 2 of 4 instances in which inadequate reliability was found (ST7-Self-centered/self-referential and ST14-Arrogant/haughty), the statements were based on the interviewer's observations of the subject's behavior. The unreliability of interviewer observations (i.e., signs) compared with patient reports has previously been noted with the Diagnostic Interview for Borderlines (Gunderson et al. 1981) and other structured interviews (Spitzer and Endicott 1968; Wing et al. 1967). We believed the unreliability observed in the other two statements, ST5-Uniqueness and ST13-Entitlement, could be traced to insufficient or unfocused probes and to ambiguous wording in the statement. Efforts to correct this have been made.

Table 6-2 shows the reliabilities for the section scores and total interview score. Subsequent trials confirmed these figures and showed that even inexperienced clinicians could become reliable in four training sessions. Pearson's r is used for section and total interview scores because they were interval data derived from summing previous statement scores. Reliability scores obtained on these variables are high (.82–.98) compared with the statements. This is because section totals represent synthetic efforts to condense the information that precedes them. High reliability in these scores is especially important because, as noted previously, the cutoffs on these section totals are used to establish the total interview score and hence diagnosis.

Comparisons between the reliability observed in the DIN and other instruments are limited. Other personality interview instruments generally have not reported interrater reliabilities on component variables. None of the Axis II interview instruments have had sufficient numbers of narcissistic subjects to test interrater reliability for this diagnosis. Using the DSM-III Axis II narcissistic criteria as a dimensional scale, an intraclass r of .94 was found on the Personality Disorder Examination (Loranger et al. 1987). Reliabilities on the DINs section totals and total interview score is even higher than those reported on the Diagnostic Interview for Borderlines (Cornell et al. 1983; Frances et al. 1984; Gunderson et al. 1981; Kroll et al. 1981; Yanchyshyn et al. 1986), which has a similar scoring system.

DEVELOPING CRITERIA FOR NARCISSISTIC PERSONALITY DISORDER

Axis II in DSM-III and DSM-III-R has used an empirical data base for some of its categories such as the antisocial, borderline, and schizotypal personality disorders. For many others, however, few or no empirical studies were available to inform the criteria selection. This was true for NPD, and the validity and reliability of criteria delineating this diagnostic category have not yet been studied (Docherty et al. 1986; Siever and Klar 1986). Our third study was conducted with the hope of providing an empirical basis for establishing the descriptive and discriminating characteristics of patients with NPD. Our goals were to determine whether a discrete group of characteristics can identify the patients who clinically are judged to have a primary diagnosis of NPD and, if this proved possible, to then determine what relationship these characteristics have to the existing DSM-III-R criteria set.

Eighty-two patients were subjects for this study. The 29 patients with NPD were compared with the ALL OTHERS group that consisted of 22 patients with general psychiatric diagnoses (without a dramatic cluster type of personality disorder) and 36 with other dramatic cluster personality disorders; i.e., borderline and antisocial diagnoses. The inclusion of these non-NPD diagnoses (confirmed by standardized interviews) ensured that the discrimination would challenge the descriptive validity of the NPD diagnosis.

Discriminating Features of NPD

Stepwise discriminant function analyses were used to compare the DIN scoring of the NPD group to that of the other patients. Table 6-3 shows the set of characteristics that were the best overall discriminators for identifying patients diagnosed as having NPD. Together, these characteristics were able to differentiate the NPD sample from the ALL OTHERS sample with 89% accuracy. The following description of each of the seven characteristics highlights nuances included in the specific inquiries on the DIN that may be clinically important for their use. Two occurred more frequently in the comparison group and are helpful by steering clinicians away from the NPD diagnosis.

1. *Superiority.* Typically, the people diagnosed as having NPD have a sustained view of themselves as better than other people, which causes them to view other people with disdain, as different from themselves, and as inferior.

2. *High achievements.* Narcissistic patients are usually talented and have had sustained periods of successful academic, employment, or creative achievement. This is frequently a source for their sense of superiority. It is also a reason why they are more apt to appear in private practice settings than in either institutions or clinics.

3. *No sustained pattern of antisocial behavior.* This characteristic was included in the DIN to help distinguish NPD patients from the antisocial patients. Its presence as one of the best overall discriminators is probably due to the high proportion of antisocial disorder personality patients in the ALL OTHER contrast group. It is important to note the NPD patients often broke laws once (or a few times) because of rage or to avoid defeat, and this characteristic would emerge as a strong discriminator in many differential diagnoses. Nevertheless, NPD patients did reveal less recurrent antisocial conduct patterns than other psychiatric patients. The only exception was heavily drug abusing NPD patients who committed crimes to finance their drug abuse.

4. *Uniqueness.* This refers to a sense of self as unique compared to other people or to a belief that few other people have much in

Table 6-3. NPD versus ALL OTHERS (stepwise discriminant function analysis)

Statement		F to enter	P for change in lambda	Standardized discriminant function coefficient
ST-6	Superiority	51.31	.001	0.66
ST-28	High achievement	18.33	.001	0.46
ST-32	Antisocial pattern	7.23	.001	0.43[a]
ST-5	Uniqueness	5.40	.001	0.34
ST-23	Emptiness	3.34	.01	−0.26
ST-22	Reactions to others' envy	2.98	.05	0.29
ST-11	Devaluation	2.20	.05	0.20

Note. Percentage correct group classification: 89%. Group centroids NPD, 1.97; ALL OTHERS, −0.81. NPD = narcissistic personality disorder; ALL OTHERS = group of patients with general psychiatric diagnoses and group of patients with other dramatic cluster personality disorders.
[a]Presence of ST-32 is scored negatively against diagnosis of NPD.

common with them. This may be apparent in often feeling misunderstood or in a feeling that their problems are so unusual that only someone very special can understand them.

5. *Lack of feelings of emptiness.* The presence of sustained emptiness actually was predominant in other psychiatric patients. This characteristic discriminated the NPD sample despite the fact that, as expected, emptiness frequently occurred in NPD patients. Here, the high frequency of borderline patients who typically complain of emptiness highlighted this characteristic. Nevertheless, this analysis shows that given a patient with a grandiose sense of superiority and uniqueness and with high achievements, the lack of emptiness can add strength to the credibility of a NPD diagnosis.

6. *Hostile suspicious reactions to others' envy.* Narcissistically disturbed patients reported histories in which they have reacted with hostility and suspicion to the perception of other people's envy toward them. They believe that because of envy other people have set out to hurt them, spoil their work, diminish their achievements, or criticize them behind their back.

7. *Devaluation/contempt.* Feelings of devaluation or contempt may occur toward many people but are especially evident toward anyone who they believe has betrayed or otherwise disappointed them. These become sustained attitudes of dislike or dismissal. Although not by itself a predominant characteristic, the fact that NPD patients do devalue others and feel contempt toward them makes this characteristic important as a discriminator in combination with the others mentioned previously.

Discriminant function analyses help to ensure that the included variables add discrimination. Which variables appear are closely linked to who composes the contrast group. They do not necessarily optimally characterize the designated target sample, in this instance NPD. Because of this, we are still involved in looking at more discrete discriminant function analyses that contrast the NPD sample with general psychiatric patients and the specific diagnostic groups of borderline and antisocial patients. Synthesizing these various analyses will help lead to a criteria set that optimally balances characterization and discrimination.

Of particular interest is the performance of current DSM-III-R criteria. In the *t* test comparison, five of the DSM-III-R criteria were among the list of 14 characteristics that were significantly more prevalent in the NPD group than in the comparison group (Table 6-4). These included all three of the DSM-III-R criteria that were part of the grandiosity section (exaggeration of talents, grandiose fantasies, and belief in uniqueness). The other two criteria were needs attention/admiration and entitlement from the interpersonal relations section. All five of these DSM-III-R criteria also emerged in the earlier study (Table 6-1) and may represent the best of the current criteria. Yet, the discriminant function analysis included only 1 of 9 criteria for NPD in DSM-III-R, i.e., uniqueness. The failure for the DSM-III-R criteria to appear in this analysis undoubtedly reflects an extensive conceptual and clinical overlap in the existing DSM-III-R criteria. This is a virtue insofar as it reflects criteria that surround a central core personality type. However, we expect that the ongoing analyses from this study will point to ways in which more independent criteria could add discriminating power.

SUMMARY

These studies, despite their limitations, have shown that it is possible to reliably identify patients with NPD and discriminate them with high accuracy from a mixed group of patients with related personality disorders and other psychiatric disturbances. These facts give descrip-

Table 6-4.   Comparison of NPD versus ALL OTHERS (t test)

Statement[a]		Corresponding DSM-III-R criterion	P
ST-1	Exaggeration	3	.000
ST-3	Grandiose fantasies	5	.000
ST-5	Uniqueness	4	.000
ST-6	Superiority		.000
ST-8	Boastful/pretentious		.000
ST-28	High achievements		.000
ST-7	Self-centered/referential		.001
ST-14	Arrogant/haughty		.001
ST-9	Needs attention/admiration	7	.002
ST-13	Entitlement	6	.006
ST-22	Reaction to others' envy		.007
ST-2	Belief in invulnerability		.02
ST-30	Disregard for values/rules		.03
ST-31	One or a few crimes		.03

Note.   NPD = narcissistic personality disorder; ALL OTHERS = group of patients with general psychiatric diagnoses and group of patients with other dramatic cluster personality disorders.
[a]Those that were significantly more common in the NPD group.

tive validity to the syndrome and justify its use as a separate diagnostic category. Its validity by other standards awaits future studies. These studies also suggest that the most pathognomonic characteristic of patients with NPD was their grandiose self-experience, i.e., an unrealistic overvaluation of their own talents, invulnerability, uniqueness, and superiority. This is in agreement with many of the seminal descriptions of patients with NPD found in the literature (Bursten 1973; Morrison 1986).

In summation, current studies offer evidence for the descriptive validity of the narcissistic personality disorder diagnosis. Beyond this, the question of validity still awaits examination of issues such as the stability of the diagnosis, familial, social, and genetic antecedents and/or predispositions, future course, and treatment responsiveness.

REFERENCES

Akhtar S, Thomson J: Overview: narcissistic personality disorder. Am J Psychiatry 139:12–20, 1982

American Psychiatric Association: Diagnostic and Statistical Manual of Mental Disorders, 3rd Edition. Washington, DC, American Psychiatric Association, 1980

American Psychiatric Association: Diagnostic and Statistical Manual of Mental Disorders, 3rd Edition, Revised. Washington, DC, American Psychiatric Association, 1987

Baldessarini RJ, Finkelstein S, Arana GW: The predictive power of diagnostic tests and the effect of prevalence of illness. Arch Gen Psychiatry 40:569–573, 1983

Bursten B: Some narcissistic personality types. Int J Psychoanal 54:287–300, 1973

Cooper AM: Narcissism, in American Handbook of Psychiatry. Edited by Arieti S. New York, Basic Books, 1982, pp 297–316

Cornell D, Silk K, Ludolph P, et al: Test-retest reliability of the diagnostic interview for borderlines. Arch Gen Psychiatry 40:1307–1310, 1983

Docherty J, Fiester S, Shea T: Syndrome diagnosis and personality disorder, in Psychiatric Update: American Psychiatric Association Annual Review, Vol 5. Edited by Frances AJ, Hales RE. Washington, DC, American Psychiatric Press, 1986, pp 315–355

Frances A, Clarkin J, Gilmore M, et al: Reliability of criteria for borderline personality disorder: a comparison of DSM-III and the DIB. Am J Psychiatry 141:1080–1084, 1984

Gunderson J: Borderline Personality Disorder. Washington, DC, American Psychiatric Press, 1984

Gunderson J, Kolb J, Austin V: The diagnostic interview for borderline patients. Am J Psychiatry 138:896–903, 1981

Kernberg OF: Borderline Conditions and Pathological Narcissism. New York, Jason Aronson, 1975

Kernberg OF: Severe Personality Disorders. New Haven, CT, Yale University Press, 1984

Kohut H: The Analysis of the Self. New York, International Universities Press, 1971

Kohut H: The Restoration of the Self. New York, International Universities Press, 1977

Kroll J, Pyle R, Zander J, et al: Borderline personality disorder: interrater reliability of the DIB. Schizophr Bull 7:269–272, 1981

Loranger A, Susman V, Oldham J, et al: The Personality Disorder Examination: a preliminary report. J Pers Disord 1:1–13, 1987

Modell AH: A narcissistic defence against affects and the illusion of self-sufficiency. Int J Psychoanal 56:275–282, 1975

Morrison A (ed): Essential Papers on Narcissism. New York, New York University Press, 1986

Pulver SE: Narcissism: the term and the concept. J Am Psychoanal Assoc 18:319–341, 1970

Reich A: Pathological forms of self-esteem regulation, in Psychoanalytic Study of the Child, Vol 5. New York, International Universities Press, 1953, pp 205–232

Robbins M: Narcissistic personality as a symbiotic character disorder. Int J Psychoanal 63:127–148, 1982

Ronningstam E: Comparing three systems for diagnosing narcissistic personality disorder. Psychiatry 51:300–311, 1988

Ronningstam E, Gunderson JG: Narcissistic traits in psychiatric patients. Compr Psychiatry 29:545–549, 1988

Siever L, Klar H: A review of DSM-III criteria for the personality disorders, in Psychiatric Update: American Psychiatric Association Annual Review, Vol 5. Edited by Frances AJ, Hales RE. Washington, DC, American Psychiatric Press, 1986, pp 315–355

Spitzer R, Endicott J: DIAGNO: a computer program for psychiatric diagnosis utilizing the differential diagnostic procedure. Arch Gen Psychiatry 18:746–756, 1968

Wing J, Briley J, Cooper J, et al: Reliability of a procedure for measuring and classifying present psychiatric state. Br J Psychiatry 113:499–515, 1967

Yanchyshyn G, Kutcher S, Cohen C: The diagnostic interview for border-lines: reliability and validity in adolescents. J Am Acad Child Psychiatry 25:427–429, 1986

Chapter 7

Diagnostic Efficiency of DSM-III Borderline Personality Disorder and Schizotypal Disorder

Thomas H. McGlashan, M.D.
Wayne S. Fenton, M.D.

Chapter 7

Diagnostic Efficiency of DSM-III Borderline Personality Disorder and Schizotypal Disorder

DSM-III (American Psychiatric Association 1980) follows a prototypic or dimensional model of classification for borderline personality disorder (BPD) and schizotypal personality disorder (SPD). Such a system allows for the application of actuarial decision theory to various aspects of the nosologic process (Widiger and Frances 1985). For example, it is possible to determine which of any constituent criteria of the particular diagnostic set are most common in a particular population, which are the most powerful or efficient predictors of any given diagnosis, and which are the strongest discriminators between different diagnostic groups.

The important parameters of diagnostic efficiency have been elaborated recently (Baldessarini et al. 1983; Clarkin et al. 1983; Widiger et al. 1984) and are defined in Table 7-1. Briefly, the prevalence of a particular diagnosis in a specific population constitutes its *base rate*. *Sensitivity* is the conditional probability of having a

This study was supported in part by NIMH Grant MH-35174-02 and by the Fund for Psychoanalytic Research of the American Psychoanalytic Association. We thank Linda Berman for project and manuscript coordination; Pat Inana and Carol Thompson for manuscript preparation; Allison Benesch for chart abstraction and diagnostic evaluation; Renee Marshel and Victoria Solsberry for outcome evaluation; Robert Heinssen and John Bartko for statistical consultation; Lawrence Abrams, John Cook, William Flexsenhar, Kathleen Free, Lee Goldman, Anita Gonzalez, Wendy Greenspun, Brian Healy, Tom Martin, Jim Miller, Jack O'Brien, Terry Polonus, Steven Richfield, Susan Voisinet, Robert Welp, and Donald Wright for chart abstraction; Dexter M. Bullard, Jr., and Wells Goodrich for general consultation and manuscript review.

particular symptom given that the patient has the disorder. *Specificity* is the conditional probability of not having the symptom given the absence of disorder. *Positive predictive power* is the converse of sensitivity, i.e., the conditional probability of having the disorder given the symptom or combination of symptoms. *Negative predictive power* is the converse of specificity, i.e., the conditional probability of not having the disorder given the absence of the symptom.

The parameters of diagnostic efficiency have been applied in recent times to the DSM-III criteria set for BPD (Clarkin et al. 1983; Jacobsberg et al. 1986; Morey 1985; Nurnberg et al. 1987; Pfohl et al. 1986; Widiger et al. 1984, 1986, 1987) and SPD (Jacobsberg et al. 1986; Morey 1985; Pfohl et al. 1986; Widiger et al. 1986, 1987). Specific findings will be reviewed in the discussion. This study elaborates these parameters for the DSM-III BPD and SPD criteria as identified in two cohorts of inpatients from the Chestnut Lodge Follow-up Study.

Objectives of this investigation are: 1) to estimate the base rate of BPD and SPD in samples of chronically impaired long-term inpatients, 2) to find the most efficient symptoms and combination of symptoms for predicting BPD and SPD diagnoses in these populations, and 3) to determine which of the BPD and SPD criteria best discriminate between the two diagnostic entities. Furthermore, steps 1–3 are applied to different but overlapping populations: 1) the entire sample from the Chestnut Lodge Follow-up Study ($N = 532$) consisting of pure and comorbid Axis I psychotic disorders and Axis II personality disorders and 2) a smaller, more homogeneous sample ($N = 160$) without Axis I psychotic disorders. Clarkin et al. (1983) and Widiger et al. (1984) have noted that the diagnostic efficiency

Table 7-1. Diagnostic efficiency parameters

	Disorder (symptom or combination)	
	Positive	Negative
Positive	True positives A	False positives B
Negative	False negatives C	True negatives D
Total	Total positive (A + C)	Total negative (B + D)

Note. Base rate = $(A+C)/(A+B+C+D)$; sensitivity = $A/(A+C)$ probability of symptom given the diagnosis; specificity = $D/(B+D)$ probability of not having symptom, given absence of disorder; positive predictive power = $A/(A+B)$ probability of disorder, given symptom or combination of symptoms; negative predictive power = $D/(C+D)$ probability of not having disorder, given absence of symptom or combination of symptoms.

and discriminatory power of any symptom or set of symptoms depends on particular characteristics of the population under scrutiny, such as the base rate of the diagnoses in question and the similarity versus dissimilarity of the diagnostic groups in question. Markedly different diagnostic comparison groups would be expected to enhance the efficiency of criteria symptoms. We test this by calculating the efficiency parameters in populations that differ considerably in their diagnostic composition.

METHODS

The study population comes from the Chestnut Lodge Follow-up Study that has been described elsewhere (McGlashan 1984). Briefly, that study included all patients discharged from Chestnut Lodge between 1950 and 1975, and a smaller cohort of nondischarged patients from a comparable period of time. Baseline data were gathered retrospectively from extensive medical records that were transposed onto a 25-page document called the Clinical Chart Abstract (blank forms available on request). From this document each patient was rated on approximately 200 demographic, predictor, and sign and symptom variables. The interrater reliabilities achieved for these variables have been reported (McGlashan 1984). Using these ratings, patients were rediagnosed by current criteria, including DSM-III. Kappa reliability for DSM-III diagnoses of BPD and SPD were 0.72 and 0.51, respectively (McGlashan 1984). Overall, 532 patients were evaluated with this technique.

For this study, diagnoses of BPD and SPD were assigned if the patient met the particular DSM-III criteria at cutoff scores of 5 and 4, respectively. Other diagnoses, mostly of the Axis I psychoses, were defined using DSM-III criteria according to rules detailed elsewhere (McGlashan 1984). Composition of the sample by primary diagnosis was as follows: schizophrenia 35%, schizoaffective disorder 16%, schizophreniform disorder 3%, bipolar and unipolar affective disorders 15%, and nonpsychotic personality and other disorders 30%. The first sample studied in this investigation included all patients ($N = 532$). The second sample included patients with nonpsychotic and other disorders ($N = 160$).

The patients from both samples were chronically and severely ill. For the population as a whole ($N = 532$), 45% were male, 35% had been married, and all were white and from upper-middle class socioeconomic brackets (Hollingshead and Redlich 1958). The mean ages of first psychiatric symptoms and index hospitalization were 21 and 29 years old, respectively. Four of five patients came to Chestnut Lodge with a duration of illness > 2 years, having spent an average of

18 months in three previous hospitalizations. They remained in-patients at Chestnut Lodge for a mean of 40 months.

RESULTS

Frequency Distribution of DSM-III BPD and SPD Scores

Figures 7-1 and 7-2 show the frequency with which patients from the total sample ($N = 532$) met none up to all eight of the DSM-III

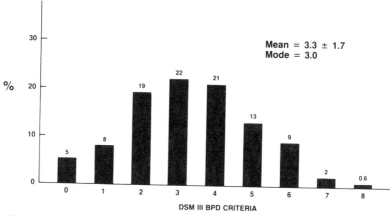

Figure 7-1. Borderline personality disorder frequency distribution of DSM-III criteria (total sample $N = 532$).

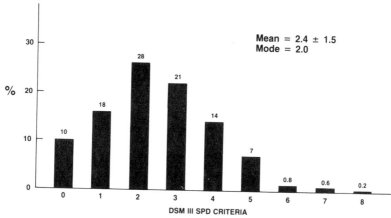

Figure 7-2. Schizotypal personality disorder frequency distribution of DSM-III criteria (total sample $N = 532$).

symptoms for BDP and SPD, respectively. On testing, the BPD distribution proved to be normal. However, SPD distribution was skewed significantly ($P < .01$), with more patients scoring in the lower range. Distributions for the smaller more homogeneous sample ($N = 160$) were the same, with BPD scores distributing normally and SPD scores skewing significantly ($P < .01$) to the right.

BPD and SPD Diagnostic Base Rates and Comorbidity Rates

Table 7-2 shows the BPD and SPD diagnostic base rates for the two samples. Patients from the total sample met the DSM-III BPD cutoff score of 5 at a rate of 24% and the DSM-III SPD cutoff score of 4 at a rate of 22%. The respective rates for the nonpsychotic sample were 31 and 11%. Seventy-six of 126 BPD cases (60%) were comorbid with an Axis I psychosis (schizophrenia, schizoaffective disorder, schizophreniform disorder, and bipolar and unipolar affective disorders) compared with 100 of the 117 SPD cases (85%). Comorbidity with other DSM-III Axis I and Axis II diagnoses could not be ascertained because chart abstracts were not scored for these conditions in the original study (McGlashan 1984).

Table 7-3 shows the rate of diagnostic overlap between BPD and SPD for the two samples. In the total sample, the rate of BPD and SPD comorbidity ($N = 33$) was equivalent between the BPD category (33 of 126 [26%]) and the SPD category (33 of 117 [28%]). In the nonpsychotic sample, the rate of BPD and SPD comorbidity ($N = 7$) was low for BPD (7 of 50 [14%]) but substantial for SPD (7 of 17 [41%]).

Base Rates, Diagnostic Efficiency, and Discriminating Power of DSM-III BPD Symptoms

Table 7-4 presents the nosologic parameters of the eight DSM-III BPD criteria for the two samples. This includes base rates; diagnostic

Table 7-2. BPD and SPD base rates

	DSM-III BPD		DSM-III SPD	
	n	%	n	%
Total sample ($N = 532$)	126	23.7	117	21.9
Nonpsychotic sample ($N = 160$)	50	31.3	17	10.6

Note. BPD = borderline personality disorder; SPD = schizotypal personality disorder.

efficiency measures of sensitivity, specificity, positive predictive power, and negative predictive power; and the point biserial correlation (r) of each symptom with total BPD and SPD scale score (exclusive of the symptom being examined). The latter measure allows for a determination of the association and specificity between the symptom and syndrome.

Symptom base rates were comparable between the two samples and ranged widely. Intolerance of aloneness was the least frequently occurring symptom and unstable relationships the most frequently occurring symptom in both samples.

Each of the diagnostic efficiency contingent probabilities provides measures of interest, but we focus here on the symptom with the best positive predictive power. This belonged to affective instability for both samples. The symptom unstable relationships, with the highest sensitivity, was also the least specific because its presence was ubiquitous in both populations (high base rates). On the other hand, affective instability had a low base rate and high specificity in both samples, thus enhancing its positive predictive power.

Positive predictive power in Table 7-4 presents the conditional probabilities of meeting the full DSM-III BPD diagnosis given each of the eight individual BPD symptoms. We also tested whether combinations of symptoms might be more efficient by calculating positive predictive power and sensitivity for each possible combination of two and three symptoms. There are 28 possible two-symptom combinations and 56 possible three-symptom combinations. We used sensitivity rather than negative predictive power because with combinations base rates dropped rapidly. Thus, a particular combination

Table 7-3. BPD and SPD overlap

Total sample (N = 532)		SPD		
		No	Yes	
	No	322	84	406
BPD	Yes	93	33	126
		415	117	532
Nonpsychotic sample (N = 160)		SPD		
		No	Yes	
	No	100	10	110
BPD	Yes	43	7	50
		143	17	160

Note. BPD = borderline personality disorder; SPD = schizotypal personality disorder.

Table 7-4. DSM-III BPD criteria, base rates, sensitivity, specificity, positive and negative predictive power, and correlation with diagnosis

Symptom	Total sample (N = 532)					r		Nonpsychotic sample (N = 160)					r	
	BR	SEN	SPEC	PPP	NPP	BPD	SPD	BR	SEN	SPEC	PPP	NPP	BPD	SPD
Identity disturbance	52	84	58	38	92	.22*	.16*	58	82	54	45	87	.15**	.21***
Unstable relationships	76	98	32	31	99	.27*	−.01	83	100	26	38	100	.24***	−.11
Impulsivity	54	93	59	41	96	.32*	−.09**	72	92	37	40	91	.17**	−.08
Inappropriate anger	43	78	68	43	91	.26*	.09**	46	72	64	47	83	.20****	.18**
Self-damaging acts	47	78	63	39	90	.18*	−.05	52	86	64	52	91	.18**	−.02
Affective instability	19	50	91	62	85	.21*	.06	23	50	91	71	80	.21****	.08
Emptiness/boredom	32	58	76	43	85	.13***	.07	34	58	77	54	80	.06	.11
Intolerance of aloneness	9	20	95	54	79	.12***	−.04	9	20	96	71	73	.14	−.13

Note. BR = base rate; SEN = sensitivity; SPEC = specificity; PPP = positive predictive power; NPP = negative predictive power; r = correlation of symptom with total BPD and SPD scale score (exclusive of the symptom in question); BPD = borderline personality disorder; SPD = schizotypal personality disorder.

*P < .0001. **P < .05. ***P < .005. ****P < .01.

may be highly predictive of diagnosis but almost nonexistent in that diagnostic population. The best symptom combinations, therefore, are those with high positive predictive power that occur with reasonable frequency in the diagnostic cohort (moderate sensitivity or better). Therefore, we arbitrarily defined the most efficient symptom combination as the one with the best positive predictive power among those with a sensitivity of at least 50%. For the total sample, the best two-way combination by this convention was impulsivity and chronic emptiness/boredom (positive predictive power, 0.68; sensitivity, 0.53) and for the nonpsychotic sample it was intense anger and self-damaging acts (positive predictive power, 0.78; sensitivity, 0.58).

Three-way symptom combinations proved to be not very useful. In the total sample, while 25 of 56 possible combinations (45%) had positive predictive power of greater than 90%, their average sensitivity was only 18%.

The final two columns in Table 7-4 list the point biserial correlations of each BPD symptom with a diagnosis of BPD and SPD. We defined the symptom discriminating best between BPD and SPD as that with the largest difference in these correlations: r for BPD minus r for SPD. Using this convention, the three most discriminating symptoms for the total sample were impulsivity, unstable relations, and self-damaging acts (in that order). For the nonpsychotic sample, they were unstable relations, intolerance of aloneness, and impulsivity. Two BPD symptoms, identity disturbance and intense anger, not only failed to discriminate between BPD and SPD, but they were significantly associated with a diagnosis of SPD.

Base Rates, Diagnostic Efficiency, and Discriminating Power of DSM-III SPD Symptoms

Table 7-5 presents the nosologic parameters of the eight DSM-III SPD criteria for the two samples. Base rates varied widely within samples but were comparable across samples with the exception of suspiciousness-paranoid, which ranged from 17% in the nonpsychotic sample to 56% in the total sample. Across both samples, magical thinking was the least frequently occurring symptom. Suspicious-paranoid was the most frequently occurring symptom for the total sample and social isolation was the most frequently occurring symptom for the nonpsychotic sample. For both samples, the DSM-III SPD symptom of odd communication had the highest positive predictive power and the symptom of social isolation had the lowest positive predictive power.

Using the same convention as articulated for the BPD symptoms,

Table 7-5. DSM-III SPD criteria, base rates, sensitivity, specificity, positive and negative predictive power, and correlation with diagnosis

| Symptom | Total sample (N = 532) | | | | | | | Nonpsychotic sample (N = 160) | | | | | | |
| | | | | | | *r* | | | | | | | *r* | |
	BR	SEN	SPEC	PPP	NPP	SPD	BPD	BR	SEN	SPEC	PPP	NPP	SPD	BPD
Odd communication	23	59	88	57	88	.24*	.04	14	65	92	50	96	.25*****	−.02
Ideas of reference	21	48	87	51	86	.14**	−.08	12	47	92	42	94	.16****	.10
Suspicious/paranoid	56	87	53	34	94	.21*	−.19*	17	65	89	40	96	.25**	−.02
Illusions/ depersonalization/ derealization	16	37	89	49	83	.14**	.16*	14	29	88	23	91	.10	.26*****
Magical thinking	10	22	94	51	81	.08	.002	11	35	92	35	92	.09	−.18****
Inadequate rapport	26	56	82	47	87	.17*	.12***	19	47	84	26	93	.13	.15
Social anxiety	32	60	96	41	87	.09*****	.11****	41	88	65	23	98	.21***	.02
Social isolation	55	80	52	32	90	.12**	.04	50	65	52	14	92	.08	.03

Note. BR = base rate; SEN = sensitivity; SPEC = specificity; PPP = positive predictive power; NPP = negative predictive power; *r* = correlation of symptom with total BPD and SPD scale score (exclusive of the symptom in question); BPD = borderline personality disorder; SPD = schizotypal personality disorder.
*$P < .0001$. **$P < .005$. ***$P < .01$. ****$P < .05$. *****$P < .001$.

the best two-way combination of DSM-III SPD symptoms for the total sample was odd communication and suspicious-paranoid (positive predictive power, 0.67; sensitivity, 0.51). For the nonpsychotic sample it was odd communication and social anxiety (positive predictive power, 0.77; sensitivity, 0.59).

Sixty-six percent of the possible three-way combinations of DSM-III SPD symptoms for the total sample had positive predictive powers greater than 90%. However, their average SEN was only 10%. The three DSM-III SPD symptoms discriminating best between SPD and BPD were suspiciousness-paranoid, ideas of reference, and odd communication (in that order) for the total sample and odd communication, suspiciousness-paranoid, and magical thinking (in that order) for the nonpsychotic sample. The SPD criterion, illusions/depersonalization/derealization, had significant and larger correlations with BPD than SPD in both samples. Inadequate rapport and social anxiety also had significant positive correlations with BPD, but for the total sample only.

DISCUSSION

Methodological Shortcomings

This study was conducted on a racially and socioeconomically homogeneous population, thus limiting its demographic representativeness. Psychopathologically, most patients were severely and chronically ill, being referred to a tertiary care institution specializing in treatment resistant cases. Although this renders the results less generalizable to a large segment of psychiatric patients, the sample is representative of the chronic end of the spectrum and is one of the first such samples to be studied in this manner.

We did not test the patients for all possible DSM-III disorders. Diagnostic ratings in the original study (McGlashan 1984) were limited to Axis I psychoses and Axis II BPD and SPD. This undoubtedly resulted in an underestimate of the degree of BPD and SPD comorbidity. For example, although our rates of Axis I comorbidity were high (60% for BPD and 85% for SPD), Fyer et al. (1988) tested an inpatient sample with an expanded set of DSM-III disorders and found the BPD cohort to be comorbid in 91% of cases.

It is suggested that diagnostic efficiency parameters will vary depending on sample composition and especially on the nature of the diagnostic comparison groups (Widiger et al. 1984). This served as the rationale for our strategy of calculating diagnostic efficiency in two samples. Although these samples were quite different vis-à-vis their loading of DSM-III Axis I psychotic disorders, they were not independent; the smaller nonpsychotic sample was nested in the larger total sample. Therefore, some of the similarity of results across samples may have been influenced by this overlap. We selected our particular cohorts to be representative, on the one hand, of chronic psychiatric inpatients (total sample) and, on the other, of nonpsychotic patients with high loadings of character pathology, for whom the diagnostic efficiency of BPD and SPD has been studied most frequently.

Sign and symptom ratings based on prospective structured interviews are clearly superior to the retrospective application of criteria to clinical charts, as conducted here. The retrospective strategy is particularly vulnerable to gaps in the record, and although our overall missing information rate was only 12% (McGlashan 1984), our estimates of the presence or absence of symptoms undoubtedly erred in the direction of false negatives. The BPD symptom, intolerance of being alone, had a base rate of only 9% in both of our samples. In an interview study of 76 outpatients, Clarkin et al. (1983), found intolerance of being alone in 25% of the sample. Although their base rate was higher than ours, they found, like us, that intolerance of being alone was the least frequently occurring symptom among the BPD set. This supports the validity of our relative base rates while suggesting that their absolute values may be underestimates.

Finally, the retrospective nature of our ratings may have resulted in attenuated reliabilities. Our kappa interrater reliability for the SPD diagnosis was 0.51, which is moderate at best. Many of the criteria for this syndrome, such as magical thinking, illusions, or inadequate rapport are subtle and less easy to identify from clinical records.

Central Findings of This Study

The main findings of this study for BPD and SPD are summarized in the first two rows of Tables 7-6 and 7-7.

The distribution of BPD scores was normal but the SPD distribution skewed to the right (higher frequency at lower scores). This difference is striking but difficult to interpret. A normal segment of the BPD population could be severely or prototypically borderline, but severe or prototypic schizotypals were infrequent. Could it be that BPD is an independent entity, even when comorbid, and that patients can be very borderline without that implying or suggesting a change in diagnosis? In contrast, SPD may not be so independent; greater severity may be associated with a change in diagnosis to schizophrenia or schizoaffective disorder.

The comorbidities of both BPD and SPD for other Axis I and Axis II disorders were high, even though our rates are probably conserva-

Table 7-6. DSM-III BPD summary of literature on diagnostic efficiency

Reference	Sample and demography	Diagnostic procedure and composition	BPD base rate (%)	Comorbidity of BPD		
				Axis 1 (%)	Axis 2 (%)	SPD (%)
This study	532 long-term inpatients Race: 100% white Age: 29 years Sex: 55% female Marital status: 65% single	Retrospective chart review. Composition: DSM-III S, SA, SF, BI, UNI, SPD, BPD, other	24	60		
	160 long-term inpatients	Composition: SPD, BPD, other; excludes DSM-III Axis 1 psychoses	31	0		14
Nurnberg et al. 1987	17 short-term inpatients Race: NI Age 17–35 years Sex: 59% female Marital status: NI	Structured clinical interview. All BPD; excludes OBS, DSM-III Axis 1 psychosis, retardation, substance problems. Comparison groups: $N = 20$ with no mental illness	46 ($N = 17$)			
Widiger et al. 1986 and Widiger et al. 1987	84 short-term inpatients Race: 92% white Age: 28 ± 9 years Sex: 36% female Marital status: 45% single	Structured clinical interview. Mostly personality disorders; excludes DSM-III Axis 1 S, MAD, OBS	63 ($N = 53$)			55 ($N = 29$)

Pfohl et al. 1986	131 in- and outpatients Race: NI Age: 35 ± 14 years Sex: 76% female Marital status: NI	Structured clinical interview. Mostly personality disorders; excludes Axis 1 S, OBS, retardation, other psychoses; includes depression, anorexia, alcoholism, somatization disorder	22 with OPD (N = 29)		90 (N = 26)
					21 (N = 6)
Jacobsberg et al. 1986	64 in- and outpatients Race: NI Age: 32 years Sex: 64% female Marital status: NI	Structured clinical interview. Mostly Axis 2, excludes clear Axis 1 disorder	34 (N = 22)	0	0 with OPD
					73 (N = 16)
Morey 1985	37 long-term inpatients Race: NI Age: 19 years (range 15–29 years) Sex: 45% female Marital status: NI	Retrospective chart review. Composition: DSM-III S, BI, NPD, SPD, BPD			
Clarkin et al. 1983	76 outpatients Race: 99% white Age: early 30's Sex: about 80% female Marital status: 58% single	Structured clinical interview. Mostly personality disorders; excludes Axis 1 organic schizophrenic, affective disorder	26 (N = 20)	0	100 with OPD
					40 (N = 8)

Table 7-6. DSM-III BPD summary of literature on diagnostic efficiency (continued)

Symptom base rate		Single-symptom PPP		Two-symptom combinations	Symptom discriminators with SPD	
Highest (%)	Lowest (%)	Highest	Lowest		Best	Worst
Intense unstable relations (76)	Intolerance of being alone (9)	Affective instability (0.62)	Intense unstable relationships (0.31)	Impulsivity and chronic emptiness/boredom (PPP = 0.68, SEN = 0.53)	Impulsivity	Identity disturbance
Intense unstable relations (83)	Intolerance of being alone (9)	Affective instability (0.71) Impulsivity or intense unstable relationships (0.89)	Intense unstable relationships (0.38) Chronic emptiness/boredom (0.67)	Intense anger and self-damaging acts (PPP = 0.78, SEN = 0.58), Intense unstable relationships and impulsivity (PPP = 0.94, SEN = 0.94)	Intense unstable relationship	Identity disturbance
Intense uncontrolled anger (71)	Identity disturbance (36)	Identity disturbance (0.87) Intense unstable relationships or self-damaging acts (0.76)	Affective instability (0.74) Intolerance of being alone (0.42)		Self-damaging acts	Chronic emptiness/boredom

Impulsivity (73)	Self-damaging acts (38)	Self-damaging acts (0.63)	Impulsivity (0.38)		Intense uncontrolled anger	Chronic emptiness/boredom
Impulsivity (100)	Intolerance of being alone (25)	Intense unstable relationships (0.69)	Intolerance of being alone (0.38)	Intense unstable relationships and identity disturbance (PPP = 1.0, SEN = 0.60)	Affective instability	Identity disturbance

Note. BI = bipolar affective disorder; BPD = borderline personality disorder; MAD = major affective disorder; NI = no information; NPD = narcissistic personality disorder; OBS = organic brain syndrome; OPD = other personality disorders; PPP = positive predictive power; S = schizophrenia; SA = schizoaffective disorder; SEN = sensitivity; SF = schizophreniform disorder; SPD = schizotypal personality disorder; UNI = unipolar affective disorder.

Table 7-7. DSM-III SPD summary of literature on diagnostic efficiency

Reference	Sample and demography	Diagnostic procedure and composition	SPD base rate (%)	Comorbidity			Symptom base rate	
				Axis 1 (%)	Axis 2 (%)	BPD (%)	Highest (%)	Lowest (%)
This study	N = 532; see Table 6	See Table 7-6	22	85		28	Suspicious-paranoid (56)	Magical thinking (10)
	N = 160; see Table 6	See Table 7-6	11	0		41	Social isolation (50)	Magical thinking (11)
Widiger et al. 1986 and Widiger et al. 1987	See Table 6	See Table 7-6	57 (N = 48)			60 (N = 29)	Social anxiety (77)	Inadequate rapport (33)
Pfohl et al. 1986	See Table 6	See Table 7-6	9 (N = 12)		92 with OPD (N = 11)	50 (N = 6)		
Jacobsberg et al. 1986	See Table 6	See Table 7-6	55 (N = 35)	0	0 with OPD	46 (N = 16)	Social anxiety (92)	Illusions, depersonalization, derealization (42)
Morey 1985	See Table 6	See Table 7-6						

Table 7-7. DSM-III SPD summary of literature on diagnostic efficiency (continued)

Single-symptom PPP		Two-symptom combinations	Symptom discriminators with BPD	
Highest	Lowest		Best	Worst
Odd communication (0.57)	Social isolation (0.32)	Odd communication and suspicious-paranoid (PPP = 0.67, SEN = 0.51)	Suspicious-paranoid	Illusions, depersonalization, derealization
Odd communication (0.50)	Social isolation (0.14)	Odd communication and social anxiety (PPP = 0.77, SEN = 0.59)	Odd communication	Illusions, depersonalization, derealization
Suspicious-paranoid (0.89)	Social isolation (0.63)		Odd communication	Social anxiety
Ideas of reference (0.52)	Social anxiety (0.17)			
Inadequate rapport (0.80)	Social anxiety (0.58)		Inadequate rapport	Suspicious-paranoid
			Ideas of reference	Social anxiety

Note. BPD = borderline personality disorder; OPD = other personality disorders; PPP = positive predictive power; SEN = sensitivity; SPD = schizotypal personality disorder.

tive estimates. Such diagnostic overlap has become recognized as commonplace for BPD (Fyer et al. 1988); our findings suggest that this may be even truer for SPD. Overall, it appears that the clinician cannot stop with a diagnosis of SPD and/or BPD, but should take their presence as a signal to look for other disorders as well. For BPD and SPD from clinical samples, comorbidity appears to be the normal state of affairs.

Our rate of SPD/BPD comorbidity was substantial. In our non-psychotic sample, 41% of our schizotypal patients met criteria for BPD and 14% of our borderline patients met criteria for SPD. This unequal overlap rate is similar to several previous studies showing that being schizotypal carries with it a greater probability of also being borderline than vice versa (see the comorbidity columns of Tables 7-6 and 7-7). The rates of comorbidity were roughly equivalent in the total sample, reflecting the higher base rate of SPD in psychotic cohorts.

Clarkin et al. (1983) and Widiger et al. (1984) suggested that diagnostic efficiency conditional probabilities would increase the more dissimilar the constituent diagnostic groups of any sample. We did not find this. In fact, our diagnostic efficiency parameters were remarkably similar despite wide differences in the Axis I composition of our two samples. The comparability of our findings may have stemmed from sources of hidden homogeneity across samples, like nonindependence and/or equivalent levels of chronicity. Neverthe-less, the close replication of results in our two samples does suggest that the presence of significant Axis I psychopathology may not be as confounding as originally thought. Our findings vis-à-vis diagnostic efficiency are summarized below along with the literature to date.

Diagnostic Efficiency Parameters in This Study and the Literature

Tables 7-6 and 7-7 also contain summaries of other literature on diagnostic efficiency in BPD and SPD. Most studies are recent, and all but two have studied both BPD and SPD.

The samples in Tables 7-6 and 7-7 cover a wide range, from outpatients to mixed groups of inpatients and outpatients to short-term inpatients to long-term inpatients. Most cohorts were white with variable ages, sex distributions, and marital statuses. With the excep-tion of our total sample ($N = 532$), all cohorts were primarily charac-ter disordered without Axis I comorbidity (especially psychosis).

In Table 7-6, the BPD base rates range between 25% and 33% of each sample. BPD comorbidity with Axis II other personality disor-ders ranged from 0 to 100%; comorbidity with SPD was ubiquitous, but not consistent in range.

The diagnostic efficiency parameters for BPD were highly variable across studies. For example, unstable relations had the highest positive predictive power in three studies (Clarkin et al. 1983; Nurnberg et al. 1987; Pfohl et al. 1986), but had the lowest positive predictive power in our two samples. Affective instability, on the other hand, had the highest positive predictive power in our two samples, but scored lowest in the Widiger et al. (1986) sample. Positive predictive power absolute values also varied widely. Symptoms with the best positive predictive power in each study had values ranging between 0.63 and 0.89, whereas symptoms with the lowest positive predictive power had values ranging between 0.31 and 0.74. Therefore, a symptom with the lowest positive predictive power in one sample could have a higher value than a symptom with the highest positive predictive power in another sample. Also, the best two-symptom combinations were not consistent, although as a general rule, positive predictive power increased and sensitivity decreased as more symptoms were combined. Finally, the symptoms that discriminated best between BPD and SPD also changed from study to study. In fact, each of the five investigations studying this dimension came up with a different BPD symptom that was the most discriminating. The worst discriminators were more consistent: identity disturbance in three studies and chronic emptiness/boredom in two studies.

A previous study from the Chestnut Lodge follow-up (McGlashan 1987; not shown in tables) compared the frequency of symptoms across three Axis II cohorts; SPD ($N = 10$), BPD ($N = 81$), and comorbid SPD/BPD ($N = 18$). These groups were constructed differently than the groups in this study. SPD groups were defined with DSM-III SPD criteria at cutoff scores of 4 and 3 and BPD groups were defined with DSM-III BPD criteria at cutoff scores of 5 and 4 and/or Gunderson and Kolb (1978) BPD criteria at cutoff scores of 7 and 6. Straight comparison of symptom frequency across groups in that study revealed that the most discriminating BPD symptoms were unstable relations, impulsivity, and self-damaging acts, whereas the least discriminating symptoms were intense anger and intolerance of aloneness. In contrast, this study applied diagnostic efficiency parameters to the same overall sample but from which BPD and SPD groups were constructed solely using DSM-III at conventional cutoff levels. Tested in this fashion, unstable relations remained the most discriminating symptom between BPD and SPD in the nonpsychotic sample, but it achieved the lowest positive predictive power in both samples.

From Table 7-7, it is clear that for SPD across studies, base rates varied considerably as did comorbidity with other personality disorders, whereas comorbidity with BPD was consistent at 50%. By diagnostic efficiency measures, social-interpersonal SPD items (social anxiety and social isolation) had higher base rates but less positive predictive power for SPD and less discriminatory power between SPD and BPD than did cognitive-perceptual SPD items (ideas of reference, suspicious-paranoid, and magical thinking). This supports the psychometric usefulness of the cognitive-perceptual SPD criteria in clinical populations as reported recently by Widiger et al. (1987).

Straight comparison of symptom frequencies from our previous study (McGlashan 1987) revealed that the most discriminating SPD symptoms were odd communication, suspicious-paranoid, and social isolation, whereas the least discriminating symptom was illusions/depersonalization/derealization. In contrast, the study of diagnostic efficiency parameters found social isolation to have the lowest positive predictive power. However, illusions/depersonalization/derealization continued to show the lowest discriminatory power between SPD and BPD.

CONCLUSION

Overall, we are struck with the enormous variability of results across samples and within samples depending on the testing procedures applied (straight frequency count versus diagnostic efficiency count). Furthermore, it is difficult to ascertain any relationship(s) between diagnostic efficiency results summarized in Tables 7-6 and 7-7, and the sample compositions, demographics, or the varying degrees of SPD and BPD base rates and comorbidity rates. Such relationships may exist, but their demonstration will require more study and empirical testing across various samples. For now, this heterogeneity of findings cautions for the retention and further scrutiny of most BPD and SPD criteria and cautions against the exclusion of any criteria, with the possible exceptions of intolerance of aloneness for BPD and of illusion/depersonalization/derealization for SPD. By default, the lack of consistent findings thus far supports most BPD and SPD criteria as originally chosen for DSM-III.

REFERENCES

American Psychiatric Association: Diagnostic and Statistical Manual of Mental Disorders, 3rd Edition. Washington, DC, American Psychiatric Association, 1980

Baldessarini RJ, Finkelstein S, Arana GW: The predictive power of diagnostic tests and the effect of prevalence of illness. Arch Gen Psychiatry 40:569–573, 1983

Clarkin JF, Widiger TA, Frances A, et al: Prototypic typology and the borderline personality disorder. J Abnorm Psychol 92:263–275, 1983

Fyer MR, Frances AJ, Sullivan T, et al: Comorbidity of borderline personality disorder. Arch Gen Psychiatry 45:348–352, 1988

Hollingshead AB, Redlich FC: Social Class and Mental Illness. New York, John Wiley, 1957

Jacobsberg LB, Hymowitz P, Barasch A, et al: Symptoms of schizotypal personality disorder. Am J Psychiatry 143:1222–1227, 1986

McGlashan TH: The Chestnut Lodge follow-up study, I: follow-up methodology and study sample. Arch Gen Psychiatry 41:573–585, 1984

McGlashan TH: Testing DSM-III symptom criteria for schizotypal and borderline personality disorders. Arch Gen Psychiatry 44:143–148, 1987

Morey LC: A psychometric analysis of five DSM-III categories. Pers Individ Differ 6:323–329, 1985

Nurnberg HG, Hurt SW, Feldman A, et al: Efficient diagnosis of borderline personality disorder. J Pers Disord 1:307–315, 1987

Pfohl B, Coryell W, Zimmerman M, et al: DSM-III personality disorders: diagnostic overlap and internal consistency of individual DSM-III criteria. Compr Psychiatry 27:21–34, 1986

Widiger TA, Frances A: The DSM-III personality disorders. Arch Gen Psychiatry 42:615–623, 1985

Widiger TA, Hurt SW, Frances A, et al: Diagnostic efficiency and DSM-III. Arch Gen Psychiatry 43:1005–1012, 1984

Widiger TA, Frances A, Warner L, et al: Diagnostic criteria for the borderline and schizotypal personality disorders. J Abnorm Psychol 95:43–51, 1986

Widiger TA, Frances A, Trull TJ: A psychometric analysis of the social-interpersonal and cognitive-perceptual items for the schizotypal personality disorder. Arch Gen Psychiatry 44:741–745, 1987

Chapter 8

Axis I and Axis II Comorbidity Findings: Implications for Validity

Bruce Pfohl, M.D.
Donald W. Black, M.D.
Russell Noyes, M.D.
William H. Coryell, M.D.
Joseph Barrash, Ph.D.

Chapter 8

Axis I and Axis II Comorbidity Findings: Implications for Validity

Numerous studies report that comorbidity rates for personality disorders and Axis I disorders exceed chance expectations (Pfohl et al. 1984; Reich et al. 1986; Tyrer et al. 1983). Explanations for this finding include the possibilities that Axis I disorders predispose to Axis II disorders, that Axis II disorders predispose to Axis I disorders, or that some third environmental or biologic risk factor predisposes to both Axis I and Axis II disorders. It is also possible that the association is an artifact resulting from one disorder contaminating the measurement of the other. Regardless of which of these explanations are true, one fact remains the same: if the distinctions between individual DSM-III (American Psychiatric Association 1980) personality disorder categories have any validity (i.e., different antecedents and different consequences), it is reasonable to expect different personality disorders to be more prominent among patients with different Axis I diagnoses. Further, if the DSM-III multiaxial approach to diagnosis is valid, then it should be possible to demonstrate some relationship between Axis II diagnoses and the expression and course of the comorbid Axis I diagnoses. In this chapter we will review a series of comorbidity studies that addresses these points.

Except as noted, all studies that were reviewed used the Structured Interview for DSM-III Personality Disorders (SIDP) (Pfohl et al. 1982; Stangl et al. 1985). A structured approach is especially important due to the finding that personality diagnosis is often unreliable when unstructured clinical interviews are used (Mellsop et al. 1982). Furthermore, a structured approach offers some protection against the tendency for clinicians to give differential attention to the diagnostic criteria for personality disorders they feel are most likely to be associated with a given Axis I diagnosis.

The SIDP consists of a 90-minute interview of the patient followed by a 30-minute interview of a knowledgeable informant, usually a spouse, parent, or friend of several years. The interview is organized by topic rather than personality disorder, and there is complete assessment of each DSM-III personality criterion with no attempt to skip out even if most of the criteria for a given personality disorder have been judged as not present. The SIDP questions are designed to inquire about behaviors in a nonthreatening manner and are worded to address what the personality traits look like from the perspective of the individual experiencing them. Final ratings are not made until after the interview of the knowledgeable informant. Test/retest reliability is in the good to fair range for most personality disorders (Stangl et al. 1985).

AXIS II COMORBIDITY RATES AMONG SELECTED DSM-III DISORDERS

Table 8-1 describes the selection procedures for each of the comorbidity studies reviewed here. Although patients were collected as part of several separate studies, all were conducted at the University of Iowa with SIDP interviewers trained by the developers of the instrument. All studies used DSM-III criteria to identify patients with specified Axis I disorders. All studies excluded patients with a current diagnosis of schizophrenia, mental retardation, or organic brain syndrome. When the Axis I disorder was episodic, patients and knowledgeable informants were repeatedly reminded to describe what the patient is like when he or she is not in the midst of an episode.

All cases described in Table 8-1 were symptomatic with their Axis I disorders at the time of the SIDP interview. The depressed sample in Table 8-1 were hospitalized at the time of interview. The other three groups were not. However, about 66% of the obsessive-compulsive disorder (OCD) cases had been hospitalized in the past. We previously demonstrated similar rates of personality disorder with SIDP in hospitalized depressed patients and in recovered cases with a past history of depression (Zimmerman M, Pfohl B, Coryell W, et al., unpublished observations). In addition, the pattern of findings to be described argues against a conclusion that differences between groups can be explained by the fact that the hospitalized group was simply sicker and, therefore, more likely to have concurrent personality diagnoses in general.

Table 8-2 summarizes the rates of personality disorder among each of the four groups. The fact that personality diagnoses were infrequent among healthy control subjects provides some reassurance that the SIDP methodology does not make frequent personality disorder diagnoses where few diagnoses would be expected. A comparison of the three patient groups suggests that the hospitalized depressed sample is more likely to have cluster B personality diagnoses (dramatic unstable cluster), whereas the OCD and panic disorder cases are more likely to meet criteria for the cluster C diagnoses (anxious fearful cluster). It also appears that OCD patients are more likely to receive personality diagnoses from cluster A (the odd, eccentric cluster) than either of the other two patient groups.

Because personality diagnoses are not mutually exclusive, it is not possible to conduct a χ^2-analysis to compare the pattern for the entire table in one test. Statistical comparison of individual personality diagnoses was conducted with the χ^2-test after making the following

Table 8-1. Source and characteristics of patient samples discussed in this chapter

Source	Sample size	Female (%)	Age
Major depression (Pfohl, Stangl, and Zimmerman 1984) Consecutive admissions to a general adult inpatient unit meeting DSM-III criteria for major depression without psychosis or organic brain syndrome	78	69	35 ± 15
Obsessive-compulsive disorder (Pfohl, Black, and Noyes, unpublished data) Outpatients located by advertisements and word of mouth to participate in a clomipramine drug trial. Had to meet DSM-III-R criteria and not have psychosis or organic brain syndrome	37	60	37 ± 10
Panic disorder (Reich and Noyes 1987) Outpatients located by advertisements and word of mouth to participate in a drug treatment trial for panic disorder	83	59	35 ± 12
Healthy control subjects (Coryell and Zimmerman, unpublished data) Responders to a newspaper ad asking for healthy volunteers. All cases had no history of psychiatric diagnosis by SADS interview	35	62	38 ± 10

Note. All values are presented as percentage or means ± SD as appropriate.

Table 8-2. Rates of personality disorder among cohorts of patients with different Axis I diagnoses[a]

	Healthy control subjects (N = 35)		Major depression (N = 78)		Obsessive-compulsive (N = 37)		Panic disorder (N = 83)	
Cluster A								
Paranoid personality disorder	0	0%	1	1%	7	19%	5	6%[b]
Schizoid personality disorder	0	0%	1	1%	0	0%	0	0%[b]
Schizotypal personality disorder	1	3%	7	9%	7	19%	0	0%[b]
Cluster B								
Histrionic personality disorder	1	3%	14	18%	4	11%	9	10%
Narcissistic personality disorder	1	3%	0	0%	2	5%	0	0%
Antisocial personality disorder	0	0%	1	1%	0	0%	1	1%
Borderline personality disorder	0	0%	18	23%	7	19%	6	7%[c]
Cluster C								
Avoidant personality disorder	0	0%	12	15%	10	27%	18	20%
Dependent personality disorder	0	0%	13	17%	17	46%	16	18%[d]
Compulsive personality disorder	2	3%	5	6%	11	30%	7	8%[d]
Passive-aggressive personality disorder	3	9%	3	4%	18	49%	2	2%[d]

[a] All statistical comparisons omit healthy control subjects and consist of a χ^2-comparison of frequency of specified personality diagnosis across three patient groups with 2. [b] Test was significant at $P < .01$ for a pooled comparison of presence or absence of any cluster A diagnoses. [c] Frequency of personality disorder diagnosis differed significantly at $P < .05$. [d] Frequency of personality disorder diagnosis differed significantly at $P < .001$.

adjustments. First, the control group was excluded from analysis because a finding of few personality disorders in healthy control subjects merely supports the conclusion that healthy control subjects have less personality psychopathology in general, and does not argue for differential comorbidity among patients with different Axis I psychopathology. Personality diagnoses with cell sizes < 5 were excluded to satisfy restrictions inherent in the χ^2-statistic. Because this would have excluded cluster A altogether, the three cluster A diagnoses were combined. As shown in Table 8-2, statistically significant differences were detected for cluster A as a group, and for histrionic, borderline, dependent, and compulsive personality disorders.

It is interesting to consider whether the findings in Table 8-2 can be understood in terms of the known symptomatology of Axis I disorders. For example, the low rate of borderline personality disorders (BPDs) among panic disorder patients is not surprising. These patients are frequently observed to develop phobic avoidance and a fear of embarrassing themselves in public which would preclude much of the impulsive and dramatic behavior that characterizes patients with BPD. In contrast, BPD should be more common among depressed patients, because BPD patients frequently engage in behaviors that threaten their social support system, leading to depression. Frequent suicidal behavior increases the chance that these patients will be referred to a psychiatrist.

It is harder to explain why BPD was almost as frequent among OCD patients (19%) as depressed patients (23%). This finding is probably an artifact of the small sample size, because an ongoing multicenter study of OCD (of which this sample is a part) has found that only about 11% of OCD patients studied so far meet criteria for BPD. Even this rate is surprisingly high, because the instability and impulsiveness usually attributed to BPD would seem incompatible with the rigidity and protracted decision making usually associated with OCD. The overlap between such theoretical opposites may indicate the false-positive rate for BPD attributable to the nonspecific influence of pervasive and chronic psychological distress on the assessment of the operational criteria for BPD.

The finding that patients with OCD are at increased risk for compulsive personality disorder may be explained by the fact that several of the criteria are extensions of behaviors common to OCD patients, e.g., indecisiveness and preoccupation with trivial details. It is tempting to speculate on whether a compulsive spectrum disorder analogous to the schizophrenia spectrum disorder exists (Pfohl and Andreasen 1986). A more convincing argument for the validity of such a spectrum could be made if increased risk for compulsive personality disorder could be demonstrated among first-degree relatives of OCD patients. Such a study should compare OCD relatives with relatives of patients who have another psychiatric disorder to establish the specificity of the compulsive personality disorder diagnosis.

DSM-III specified that passive-aggressive personality disorder should only be diagnosed when no other personality disorder is present. This exclusion rule was omitted in DSM-III-R (American Psychiatric Association 1987) and was not followed in the three studies reviewed here. OCD patients had the highest rate of this diagnosis. As with the case of compulsive personality disorder, this may represent an expression of OCD symptoms rather than an independent diagnosis. It may be difficult to sort out the difference between procrastination, dawdling, and stubbornness due to preoccupation with OCD symptoms, from resistance to demands expressed indirectly through procrastination and dawdling, as required by the criterion.

It is not surprising to find higher rates of dependent personality disorders among OCD patients than among healthy control subjects; however, OCD patients also received this diagnosis more often than the depressed patients. Perhaps the greater chronicity of symptoms seen among OCD patients leads many of them to seek out dependent relationships to help deal with the indecisiveness and need for reassurance so common in OCD.

IMPLICATIONS OF COMORBIDITY

The differences in distribution of individual personality diagnoses among patients with different Axis I disorders suggests that the criteria for personality disorder measure more than nonspecific psychosocial impairment. However, if the presence of such personality diagnoses is more than an artifact, the personality diagnoses should explain variations in the antecedents, course, and outcome of the Axis I disorder that are not accounted for by Axis I diagnoses alone.

Table 8-3 summarizes data from an earlier report on the sample of depressed inpatients described in Table 8-1. Patients with depression plus a personality disorder differed from patients with depression alone in having a younger age of onset of depression, poorer social support, and more severe stressful life events preceding admission. They were less likely to be dexamethasone suppression test nonsuppressors and less likely to show a 50% drop in their Hamilton Rating Scale scores by time of discharge. A 6-month follow-up study showed that the presence of personality disorder criteria continued to predict a worse course for patients with depression (Pfohl et al. 1984). These findings regarding personality and depression are in agreement with many other investigators (Akiskal et al. 1980; Black et al. 1988; Pilkonis and Frank 1988; Tyrer et al. 1983).

Personality symptoms may also predict a poor treatment response for other Axis I disorders. Preliminary results for a cohort of OCD patients (a subset of those described in Table 8-1) treated with clomipramine found that the 11 responders had significantly fewer total Axis II criteria scored positive than did the 11 nonresponders (19.6 ± 11.4 vs. 31.1 ± 11.7, $P < .05$) (unpublished data). Jenike et al. (1986) reported that only 7% of 14 OCD patients with schizotypal personality disorder vs. 90% of 26 OCD patients without schizotypal personality disorder responded to medication. Reich (1988) evaluated a series of 52 patients with panic disorder using the SIDP and found that several of the personality diagnoses predicted a poor response to benzodiazepines. Tyrer et al. (1983) reported a similar relationship between personality disorder and treatment response for several neurotic disorders using ICD-9 criteria. Studies examining categorical personality diagnosis as a predictor of psychotherapy treatment response are rare, but Turner (1987) reported that the presence of a DSM-III personality disorder predicted a worse outcome among social phobics treated with group psychotherapy.

These findings suggest that studies of Axis I disorders that ignore Axis II are just as guilty of poor design as are studies of Axis II that

Table 8-3. Differences between depressed patients with and without concurrent personality disorder diagnosis

	Depression only ($N = 37$)	Depression plus personality disorder ($N = 41$)
Age at admission	38 ± 14	33 ± 12
Female	24 (65%)	30 (73%)
Age at first episode	31 ± 13	25 ± 10[a]
Poor social support	3 (5%)	15 (36%)[b]
Axis IV (stressors)	4.3 ± 1.1	4.9 ± 1.2[a]
Abnormal DST test	15 (43%)	8 (20%)[c]
50% drop in Hamilton Rating Scale at discharge	22 (59%)	10 (24%)[d]

Note. All values are presented as number and percentage or means ± SD as appropriate. DST = dexamethasone suppression test.
[a]Student's *t* test was significant at $P < .05$. [b]χ^2 test was significant at $P < .05$. [c]Student's *t* test was significant at $P < .05$ after omiting 3 patients who did not receive a DST. [d]Student's *t* test was significant at $P < .01$.

ignore concurrent Axis I diagnoses. Because comorbid personality disorder explains considerable variance in outcome, studies that examine treatment response or course without considering Axis II as a covariate, will end up with greater unexplained error variance which translates into decreased statistical power for detecting the effects of nonpersonality variance. If there is a true interaction effect between personality and other predictor variables, the omission may result in erroneous results or discrepancies between studies with a different proportion of personality disorder cases in their populations.

AGE AND ENDURING PATTERNS OF BEHAVIOR

Because the definition of Axis II is based on enduring patterns of behavior, it is reasonable to expect that the presence of personality disorder would also relate to long-term outcome. Barrash (1988) recently completed a 3- to 4-year follow-up of the depressed sample described previously. He hypothesized that the presence of personality disorder should continue to predict a worse course and outcome even after 3 years and that the dramatic unstable cluster (cluster B) personality diagnoses would be associated with the worst prognosis. Initial analysis of the 64 patients available more than 3 years after admission failed to support either hypothesis. However, acting on the assumption that personality disorder may not be stable during the late teens and early 20s Barrash reanalyzed the data using only the 47 cases who were over 25 years of age at the time of the SIDP interview. Both hypotheses were supported by this analysis. Personality disorder, prospectively assessed 3–4 years earlier, was associated with a worse course and outcome in patients with major depression. Furthermore, it was the cluster B personality diagnoses that accounted for most of the variance. Not only was this not found in patients younger than age 25, but the trends were in the opposite direction.

Barrash (1988) reanalyzed data published by Pope et al. (1983) and found that personality disorder predicted future problems with depression in older but not younger adults. Hirschfeld et al. (1989) have reported data from a large collaborative study that assessed personality in first-degree relatives of depressed patients. A 6-year follow-up of these individuals showed that prospectively assessed personality problems predicted future onset of depression but only in relatives older than 30 years of age at the time of personality testing. It may be that the criteria for personality disorder are more subject to false positives in patients less than 25 years of age. Perhaps the criterion behaviors are not stable in cohorts of patients younger than age 25. In any case, future studies examining the implications of personality disorder diagnoses must consider age as an effect modifier.

VALIDITY OF INDIVIDUAL PERSONALITY DISORDERS

Although it has been relatively easy to demonstrate predictive validity for presence or absence of personality disorder in general, it is more difficult to show specificity for individual personality disorders. The Barrash study found some specificity for cluster B diagnoses taken as a group but a concurrent diagnosis of histrionic personality disorder should have different implications than a diagnosis of some other personality disorder. The first problem with establishing such a specific effect is the high degree of overlap between personality disorders. For example, up to 66% of BPD patients also meet criteria for histrionic personality disorder and vice versa (Pfohl et al. 1986; Pope et al. 1983). One way of dealing with this problem is to compare patients with a given diagnosis with patients with any other personality diagnoses. Table 8-4 shows what happens when this is done for histrionic personality disorder. The sample consists of depressed inpatients selected according to the description in Table 8-1. The differences in Table 8-4 are not significant. Although the results might

Table 8-4. Comparison of depressed inpatients with histrionic personality disorder versus depressed inpatients with one or more other personality disorders

	Histrionic personality disorder ($N = 29$)		Any other personality disorder ($N = 48$)	
History of dysthymia	7	21%	10	20%
Poor social support	8	28%	15	31%
History of separation/ divorce	8	28%	21	43%
Nonserious suicide attempts	14	47%	15	31%
Stressful life events	16	55%	23	48%
50% drop in Hamilton Rating Scale at discharge	14	48%	22	46%

Note. All values presented as number and percentage. None of the differences reach statistical significance by χ^2 analysis.

be different when a larger sample size is available, comparison of other individual personality disorders have yielded similar results (unpublished data).

For the most part, the data do not exist to validate that specific personality disorders as defined in DSM-III have different implications that separate the personality disorders from one another. Most studies of personality disorder have not been designed to examine specificity. For example, many of the studies reporting increased rates of schizotypal personality disorder in relatives of schizophrenic subjects fail to examine whether the rates of other personality disorders are elevated in family members of schizophrenic subjects or whether schizotypal personality disorder is elevated in relatives of patients with other Axis I disorders (Baron et al. 1983; Kendler 1988). Many of the outcome studies of BPD fail to systematically assess for other personality disorders (Tarnopolsky and Berelowitz 1987). Personality disorder researchers will need to assess a wider range of personality disorders and criteria to better assess the specificity of current criteria and to point the way to better approaches that can reduce the overlap between different personality disorder diagnoses.

AXIS I DISORDERS AS CONFOUNDERS OF AXIS II MEASUREMENT

Although the data presented so far support that comorbid Axis II diagnoses possess predictive validity, the question remains as to whether personality disorder ratings truly represent enduring patterns of behavior that persist even when Axis I symptoms are absent. Problems with Axis I state changes have been shown to bias several self-rating scales (Hirschfeld et al. 1983; Reich et al. 1986). One method of examining this question using the SIDP interview methodology is to compare the personality disorder diagnosis obtained from the patient interview during an episode of major depression with the diagnosis based on an interview with a knowledgeable informant who theoretically is better able to provide an objective view of the patient's behavior prior to the acute episode.

We previously reported such a comparison of patient versus informant interviews with 66 inpatients with major depression who were interviewed during their first week of hospitalization (Zimmerman et al. 1988). The interviews were conducted independently and blindly by two separate interviewers. During the SIDP interview, both the patient and knowledgeable informant were given the standard SIDP instructions to think about and describe examples of the target behaviors during times other than when the subject is hospitalized or suffering from some episodic condition. To the extent that our subject interview methodology was biased by the subject's depressed state, we would expect that the subject interview would be more likely to yield Axis II diagnoses than the informant interview.

Summing across all personality disorders, a mean of 17.1 ± 13.4 criteria were rated positive based on subject interview, and 23.0 ± 15.1 were rated positive based on informant interview ($P < .001$). Of the 11 DSM-III Axis II diagnoses, only one was made more frequently from subject interviews than from informant interviews. The exception was antisocial personality disorder. This may be due to the fact that the criteria for antisocial personality disorder require detailed knowledge of the individual's childhood history. The knowledgeable informant was often a spouse or confidant who did not know the individual during childhood. In any case, there is little evidence of state-related subject bias (in the hypothesized direction) using the informant interview as the reference.

In a previously unpublished study, we investigated state-related personality assessment bias in depression by repeating the SIDP 6 months later in a subset of the depressed inpatients. Thirty-six patients completed the 6-month SIDP reinterview. Informants were used for both the initial and follow-up interviews. Because some of the patients lived a considerable distance from the hospital, about half of the 6-month follow-up interviews were conducted by telephone.

Table 8-5 shows the results for all personality disorders diagnosed at least four times by either rater. The kappas range from 0.16 to 0.84. In most cases there was only a weak trend for a greater likelihood of diagnosis during the hospitalization interview than during the follow-up interview. BPD and histrionic personality disorder were actually more often diagnosed at follow-up. Schizotypal and passive-aggressive personality disorders were more often diagnosed during hospitalization and had low reliability. Schizotypal personality disorder may be one disorder that does not lend itself to telephone interview because several of the interpersonal items benefit from direct observation. The low reliability for passive-aggressive personality disorder may relate to the fact that the criteria require the interviewer to assess the motivation for the behavior.

Because validity is so closely tied to reliability, it is important to keep in mind that reliability is not a statistic attached to a specific interview, but rather reliability is a function of the interview, the interviewers, overall methodology, and the specific population being studied. The data in Table 8-5 should probably be viewed as worst case reliability estimates because: 1) time one interviews were conducted during the first week of hospitalization for depression, 2) 6–12 months passed between interviews, 3) many of the follow-up interviews were conducted by telephone, and 4) the rater at time two did not have access to historical information from the patient's chart due to the need to maintain blindness. However, the results in Table 8-5 suggest that within the constraints of the current methodology many Axis II personality diagnoses are at least moderately stable over time, even when the initial diagnosis is made during hospitalization for depression. The methodology appears adequate for studying correlates of personality in groups of depressed patients, although clinicians

Table 8-5. Six- to 12-month test-retest reliability of SIDP Axis II diagnosis comparing an inpatient face-to-face interview during hospitalization for depression (Rater 1) with a telephone interview after discharge (Rater 2)

| | | Rater 1 | | | |
		Present	Absent	Kappa	P
Paranoid personality disorder					
Rater 2	Present	2	0	0.64 ± 0.25	.0101
	Absent	2	32		
Schizotypal personality disorder					
Rater 2	Present	1	1	0.22 ± 0.32	.5057
	Absent	4	30		
Antisocial personality disorder					
Rater 2	Present	3	0	0.84 ± 0.16	.0001
	Absent	1	32		
Borderline personality disorder					
Rater 2	Present	5	3	0.58 ± 0.18	.0015
	Absent	2	26		
Histrionic personality disorder					
Rater 2	Present	5	4	0.46 ± 0.18	.0118
	Absent	3	24		
Passive-aggressive personality disorder					
Rater 2	Present	1	2	0.16 ± 0.31	.6089
	Absent	4	29		

Note. SIDP = Structured Interview for DSM-III Personality Disorders.

should exercise caution in reaching conclusions about individual patients.

SUMMARY

The data reviewed here suggest that comorbid personality diagnoses in patients with Axis I disorders have important clinical implications. The distribution of Axis II diagnoses appears to differ with different patient populations. Several studies support that presence of a personality disorder predicts a worse course and poorer response to treatment of the Axis I disorder. It is more difficult to demonstrate that different personality disorders have different implications for patients with Axis I diagnoses.

Investigators studying Axis I disorders need to recognize that personality disorder may account for a significant amount of the variance and that the implications of Axis II diagnoses may vary with age. With structured interviews it is possible to achieve at least moderate interrater reliability and stability of personality diagnoses over time. Hopefully, the growing interest in personality assessment will result in even better methodology and improvements in both reliability and validity of diagnoses.

REFERENCES

Akiskal HS, Rosenthal TL, Haykal RF, et al: Characterological depressions: clinical and sleep EEG findings separating subaffective dysthymias from character spectrum disorders. Arch Gen Psychiatry 37:777–783, 1980

American Psychiatric Association: Diagnostic and Statistical Manual of Mental Disorders, 3rd Edition. Washington, DC, American Psychiatric Association, 1980

American Psychiatric Association: Diagnostic and Statistical Manual of Mental Disorders, 3rd Edition, Revised. Washington, DC, American Psychiatric Association, 1987

Baron M, Gruen R, Asnis L, et al: Familial relatedness of schizophrenia and schizotypal states. Am J Psychiatry 140:1437–1442, 1983

Barrash J: Unstable Personality Disorders in Major Depression: Implications for Long-Term Outcome. Unpublished doctoral dissertation, Department of Psychology, University of Iowa, 1988

Black DW, Bell S, Hulbert J, et al: The importance of Axis II in patients with major depression: a controlled study. J Affective Disord 14:115–122, 1988

Hirschfeld RMA, Klerman GL, Clayton PJ, et al: Assessing personality: effects of the depressive state on trait measurement. Am J Psychiatry 140:695–699, 1983

Hirschfeld R, Klerman GL, Lavori P, et al: First onset of major depression: personality patterns. Arch Gen Psychiatry 46:345–350, 1989

Jenike MA, Baer L, Minichiello WE, et al: Concomitant obsessive-compulsive disorder and schizotypal personality disorder. Am J Psychiatry 143:530–532, 1986

Kendler KS: Familial aggregation of schizophrenia and schizophrenia spectrum disorders: evaluation of conflicting results. Arch Gen Psychiatry 45:377–383, 1988

Mellsop G, Varghese F, Joshua S, et al: The reliability of Axis II of DSM-III. Am J Psychiatry 139:1360–1361, 1982

Pfohl B, Andreasen NC: Schizophrenia: diagnosis and classification, in Psychiatry Update: American Psychiatric Association Annual Review, Vol 5. Edited by Frances AJ, Hales RE. Washington, DC, American Psychiatric Press, 1986, pp 7–24

Pfohl B, Stangl D, Zimmerman M: The Structured Interview for DSM-III Personality Disorders (SIDP). Department of Psychiatry, University of Iowa, Iowa City, IA, 1982

Pfohl B, Stangl D, Zimmerman M: The implication of DSM-III personality disorders for patients with major depression. J Affective Disord 7:309–318, 1984

Pfohl B, Coryell W, Zimmerman M, et al: DSM-III personality disorders: diagnostic overlap and internal consistency of individual DSM-III criteria. Compr Psychiatry 27:21–34, 1986

Pilkonis PA, Frank E: Personality pathology in recurrent depression: nature, prevalence, and relationship to treatment response. Am J Psychiatry 145:435–441, 1988

Pope HG, Jonas LM, Hudson JI, et al: The validity of DSM-III borderline personality disorder: a phenomenologic, family history, treatment response, and longterm follow-up study. Arch Gen Psychiatry 40:23–30, 1983

Reich J: DSM-III personality disorders and the outcome of treated panic disorder. Am J Psychiatry 145:1149–1152, 1988

Reich J, Noyes R: A comparison of DSM-III personality disorders in acutely ill panic and depressed patients. Journal of Anxiety Disorders 1:123–131, 1987

Reich J, Noyes R, Coryell W, et al: The effect of state anxiety on personality measurement. Am J Psychiatry 143:760–763, 1986

Stangl D, Pfohl B, Zimmerman M, et al: A structured interview for DSM-III personality disorders. Arch Gen Psychiatry 42:591–596, 1985

Tarnopolsky A, Berelowitz M: Borderline personality: a review of recent research. Br J Psychiatry 151:724–734, 1987

Turner RM: The effects of personality disorder diagnosis on the outcome of social anxiety symptom reduction. J Pers Disord 1:136–143, 1987

Tyrer P, Casey P, Gall J: Relationship between neurosis and personality disorder. Br J Psychiatry 142:404–408, 1983

Zimmerman M, Pfohl B, Coryell W, et al: Diagnosing personality disorder in depressed patients: a comparison of patient and informant interviews. Arch Gen Psychiatry 45:733–737, 1988

Chapter 9

Comorbidity Among Axis II Disorders

Thomas A. Widiger, Ph.D.
Allen J. Frances, M.D.
Monica Harris, Ph.D.
Lawrence B. Jacobsberg, M.D.
Minna Fyer, M.D.
Donna Manning, M.D.

Chapter 9

Comorbidity Among Axis II Disorders

Our chapter is concerned with comorbidity among the DSM-III-R (American Psychiatric Association 1987) personality disorders. Comorbidity is interpreted as the co-occurrence of independent disorders. Comorbidity is of substantial clinical and theoretical importance as the presence of one disorder can markedly affect the treatment, course, and phenomenology of another. For example, a borderline histrionic will suggest a different course and treatment than a histrionic without borderline traits (Millon 1981), and research results on borderline personality disorder (BPD) will at times be due to the presence of a comorbid personality disorder, such as antisocial personality disorder (APD) or histrionic personality disorder (HPD) (Widiger et al. 1986b). The extent and pattern of comorbidity will also indicate areas of overlap and redundancy among the diagnoses and suggest possible dimensions that might underlie the categorical taxonomy.

However, interpreting comorbidity is difficult because it might not reflect a co-occurrence of independent disorders. It can also reflect a common underlying etiology, a causal relationship between them, or a definitional artifact resulting from shared diagnostic criteria. Comorbidity can be exaggerated in settings populated by persons with the most severe forms of the disorder (Boyd et al. 1984; Fyer et al. 1988). A diagnostic system can increase comorbidity by delineating many new diagnoses, emphasizing multiple diagnoses rather than differential diagnosis, demarcating different categories along a shared spectrum of pathology, lowering the threshold for diagnosis, and including overlapping criteria (Frances et al. 1990). All of these

We thank Drs. Paul Costa and Robert McCrae for their suggestions and speculations concerning the five-factor model of personality, and Drs. Alan Dubro, Michael Lyons, and Leslie Morey for providing additional data from their studies.

methodological issues have impact on the comorbidity among personality disorders.

Twelve studies have reported data on the covariation and/or co-occurrence of all of the DSM-III-R personality disorders (Blashfield et al. 1985; Dahl 1986; Hyler and Lyons 1988; Kass et al. 1985; Livesley and Jackson 1986; Lyons et al. 1987; Millon 1987; Morey 1988; Morey et al. 1985; Pfohl et al. 1986; Widiger et al. 1987; Zanarini et al. 1987). Additional studies have reported comorbidity data on individual personality disorders, particularly BPD. Comparing and integrating this research is difficult because of the different methodologies and analyses that have been used. We will examine the findings from these studies, focusing on methodological issues that complicate this area of research, the pattern of results for BPD, schizotypal (SPD), avoidant (AVD), compulsive (CPD), and passive-aggressive (PAG) personality disorders, and the dimensions of personality that might underlie or account for the covariation among the personality disorders.

CO-OCCURRENCE

A few studies have reported co-occurrence frequencies among personality disorders. These data are informative but the results can at times be misleading. We will indicate how the frequency and percentage of co-occurrence depend substantially on the relative prevalence of the disorders within particular settings. For example, disorders with low base rates will naturally have a low number of multiple diagnoses. This can suggest little comorbidity but this low number can represent most, if not all, of the cases. For example, Dahl (1986) reported 17 cases of comorbid BPDs and SPDs in comparison to only 3 cases of comorbid dependent personality disorder (DPD) and AVD, but the 17 BPD-SPD cases accounted for only 41% of the schizotypals and 45% of the borderlines, whereas the 3 DPD-AVD cases accounted for 75% of the avoidants. The frequency of co-occurrence must always be interpreted relative to the total number of cases.

Four studies have provided enough information to calculate percentage of co-occurrence among the personality disorders (percentage of co-occurrence being equal to the number of cases that have both disorders divided by the total number of cases of either disorder). Dahl (1986) and Pfohl et al. (1986) provided the frequency of co-occurrence from which we calculated the percentages. Zanarini et al. (1987) listed the diagnoses provided by three different raters for 43 inpatients from which we calculated the percentage of co-occurrence of the diagnoses across all three raters. Morey (1988) provided the percentage of co-occurrence of DSM-III-R Axis II diagnoses. The co-occurrence rates across the four studies were normalized through arcsin transformations and then averaged (Rosenthal 1984). The results are presented in Table 9-1. Group findings were averaged rather than combining the raw data into one large data set to give equal weight to each study (Cooper 1984).

It is evident from Table 9-1 that there is considerable co-occurrence, particularly for BPD. Only one personality disorder, CPD, occurred by itself more than 25% of the time, and the percentage of time in which it did occur by itself was not very high (31%). Comorbidity would appear to be the norm in personality disorder diagnosis. The overlap in some cases was substantial, particularly for BPD and HPD (46%), BPD and APD (26%), SPD and AVD (26%), and BPD and SPD (24%). These percentages might not appear high, but a 33% co-occurrence rate would occur when half of the patients with each disorder have the other disorder (e.g., if 5 of 10 patients with disorder X have disorder Y, and 5 of 10 patients with disorder Y have disorder X, then 5 of the total of 15 patients have both disorders).

Only 4% of 196 BPD cases did not have a comorbid personality disorder. This is consistent with the reports from various studies that have assessed the comorbidity of BPD with one or more of the other personality disorders (Frances et al. 1984; Fyer et al. 1988; McGlashan 1987; Pope et al. 1983; Siever and Klar 1986). The data reported in Table 9-1 suggest that of the personality disorders, BPD is the least distinct. BPD can be differentiated from other personality disorders (Gunderson and Zanarini 1987), but even as one distinguishes BPD from one personality disorder (e.g., SPD) one is left with cases that are difficult to distinguish from other personality disorders, such as APD and HPD (Pope et al. 1983; Torgersen 1984). It is conceivable that BPD does identify a distinct personality syndrome, but co-occurrence data suggest that it rarely occurs by itself.

A limitation of the above interpretations is that the co-occurrence results depend on the prevalence of the respective disorders. It is no coincidence that the lowest co-occurrence involved those disorders with the lowest average prevalence (i.e., schizoid, paranoid, and compulsive). One can not obtain any co-occurrence when there are no cases. Averages for schizoid personality disorder (SZD) did not include results from Zanarini et al. (1987) because they did not identify any SZD cases. However, assessing co-occurrence with only one case of paranoid personality disorder (PPD) in Pfohl et al. (1986) and only one case of CPD in Dahl (1986) is almost as problematic. Co-occurrence rates can be misleading when the respective prevalence rates are substantially discrepant even if both are prevalent. The

Table 9-1. Average percentage of co-occurrence across four studies[a]

Disorder	n	Prev	Mult[b]	PPD	SZD[c]	SPD	HPD	NPD	APD	BPD	AVD	DPD	CPD
PPD	71	.07	100										
SZD	38	.05	83	3									
SPD	95	.22	84	7	9								
HPD	147	.30	83	4	1	14							
NPD	79	.10	93	2	2	8	17						
APD	67	.15	82	1	2	8	15	16					
BPD	190	.38	96	5	2	24	46	13	26				
AVD	126	.22	83	7	19	26	11	5	2	19			
DPD	99	.16	76	3	1	5	14	14	2	19	20		
CPD	36	.06	69	3	2	1	4	3	0	4	9	4	
PAG[d]	62	.15	88	12	2	1	19	10	18	18	20	15	11

Note. n = number of cases summed across four studies (N = 568); Prev = proportion of cases averaged across four studies; Mult = percentage of cases that involved a multiple diagnosis (summed rather than averaged across studies); BPD = borderline; PPD = paranoid; SZD = schizoid; SPD = schizotypal; HPD = histrionic; NPD = narcissistic; APD = antisocial; AVD = avoidant; DPD = dependent; CPD = compulsive; PAG = passive-aggressive. [a]Dahl (1986), Morey (1988), Pfohl et al. (1986), Zanarini et al. (1987). [b]Excludes Morey (1988) because necessary data not provided. [c]Excludes Zanarini et al. (1987) because no SZD cases were obtained. [d]Excludes Dahl (1986) because PAG was not diagnosed in presence of another personality disorder.

co-occurrence of HPD and narcissistic personality disorder (NPD) in Dahl (1986) was only 8%, but 100% of the three NPD patients were histrionic, whereas only 8% of the 36 HPD patients were narcissistic. Co-occurrence will always be low when one disorder is substantially more prevalent than another.

This need not be entirely artifactual. The above results for NPD-HPD do indicate that HPD often occurs without NPD. Similarly, BPD might have the highest comorbidity rate not just because it is the most prevalent: it might be comorbid and the most prevelant because its diagnostic criteria are nonspecific, perhaps identifying a level of pathology common to many of the other personality disorders (Fyer et al. 1988; Kernberg 1984). Nevertheless, substantially different prevalence rates can be misleading when the low co-occurrence of 8% for NPD-HPD (Dahl 1986) is interpreted as indicating that NPD rarely implies a comorbid diagnosis of HPD. HPD always occurred with NPD in Dahl's study.

Co-occurrence rates might change substantially when data are collected in a different setting. For example, Morey (1988) found that only 8% of 97 borderline patients were antisocial, whereas 44% of 18 antisocial patients were borderline, resulting in an overall co-occurrence of 7%. The percentage of borderline patients who were antisocial might have been much higher if the data were collected in a setting that resulted in a substantially higher prevalence of antisocial patients. Assume that the rate of 8 borderline patients for every 18 antisocial patients remains constant, then if 79 antisocial cases are added (bringing the total to 97) the co-occurrence rate increases from 7% to 23% (8 + 35 divided by 186) and the percentage of borderline patients who are antisocial increases from 8% to 33% (8 + 35 divided by 132). This assumes (perhaps falsely) that the addition of 79 antisocial cases would not also require the addition of 426 BPD cases (there were 5.39 BPD cases for every 1 APD case in the original sample), only 8% of whom would be antisocial, thereby maintaining the original co-occurrence rate.

Revisions to the criteria sets will also affect comorbidity. Morey (1988) compared the prevalence rates of DSM-III (American Psychiatric Association 1980) criteria with a 1 July 1985 draft of the DSM-III-R in the same sample of 291 subjects. The revised criteria resulted in an increased prevalence for most of the personality disorders, particularly the schizoid (an 800% increase, from a prevalence of 6% to 22%), narcissistic (350% increase, from 1.4% to 11%), paranoid (300% increase, from 7% to 22%), avoidant (240% increase, from 11% to 27%), and dependent (160% increase, from 14% to 22%). The rate for SPD decreased 185%, from 17% to 9%. The increases in prevalence resulted in increased co-occurrence because the number of subjects remained the same, with 36% of the 291 patients under DSM-III having at least one comorbid pair of diagnoses and 52% having at least one comorbid pair of diagnoses under DSM-III-R (Morey did not compare the co-occurrence rates for individual diagnostic pairs).

COVARIATION

Percentage of co-occurrence is more informative than frequency, but a seemingly high percentage of co-occurrence does not necessarily imply a significant comorbidity. Widiger et al. (1986a) reported that 55% of their BPD cases received a schizotypal diagnosis and 60% of their SDP cases received a borderline diagnosis. This might suggest a substantial comorbidity. However, the correlation in the total number of BPD and SPD symptoms possessed by each patient was only .08 ($P > .50$), suggesting little covariation (comorbidity). A χ^2 analysis of the co-occurrence rate also proved to be insignificant ($\chi^2 = .34$, $P > .50$). The reason for the appearance of inconsistency is that there was an equally substantial number of nonschizotypal patients who were borderline (67%), many nonborderline patients who were schizotypal (39%), and few cases that were neither (14%). The correlation between the presence-absence of BPD and SPD will be zero when 50% of 10 borderline patients have a SPD diagnosis and 50% of 10 schizotypal patients have a BPD diagnosis in a sample of 20 patients.

The ϕ-coefficient provides an interpretable basis for comparing results of studies that assessed co-occurrence with studies that assessed (Pearson's r) correlation in the criteria sets or the (Pearson's r) correlation in respective scales from self-report inventories (Rosenthal 1984). We calculated the ϕ-coefficient for each pair of diagnoses from the four co-occurrence studies and compared these results to covariation results based on dimensional (quantitative) ratings. Space limitations prohibit summarizing the findings for all of the diagnoses. We will discuss only BPD, SPD, AVD, CPD, and PAG, noting in particular the variation in findings across studies but also providing a meta-analytic integration of the correlations.

Borderline Personality Disorder

Table 9-2 shows results for BPD, including six co-occurrence studies that included or were confined to BPD, three that used ratings by clinicians and/or interviewers to obtain dimensional scores, and four that used scale scores from self-report inventories (the findings from the self-report inventory studies are based on results obtained from nonoverlapping scales; Widiger and Frances 1987). The studies also differed in many other respects. One sampled healthy college students

Table 9-2. Covariation of borderline with other personality disorders

Study	n	PPD	SZD[a]	SPD	HPD	NPD	APD	AVD	DPD	CPD	PAG[b]
Interview categorical											
Dahl (1986)	103	-.08	-.08	.08	.41	.11	.58	-.29	-.05	-.08	
Dubro et al. (1988)	56	-.06		-.11	.21	.41	.23	.43	.56	-.06	.10
Frances et al. (1984)	76	.10	-.08	.29	-.05	-.01	-.12	-.24	.01	-.23	-.23
Morey (1988)	291	.17	-.11	.00	.25	.15	.06	.14	.20	-.15	.02
Pfohl et al. (1986)	131	-.05	-.05	.21	.58	.28	.28	.15	.18	.04	.43
Zanarini et al. (1987)	38	.00		.29	.56	-.03	.11	.39	.33	-.16	-.10
Average		.01	-.08	.13	.35	.16	.20	.10	.21	-.11	.09
Interview dimensional											
Hyler & Lyons (1988)	358	.38	.17	.33	.38	.39	.29	.19	.19	-.08	.16
Kass et al. (1985)	609	.17	.15	.19	.26	.26	.26	.19	.14	-.05	.16
Widiger et al. (1987)	84	.18	-.28	.08	.50	.08	.43	.40	.37	-.01	.22
Average		.24	.20	.20	.39	.25	.33	.26	.22	-.05	.18
Inventory dimensional											
Livesley et al. (1986)	115	.70	.44	.62	.51	.57	.64	.63	.60	.11	.69
Lyons et al. (1987)	552	.61	.33	.69	.66	.60	.58	.54	.58	.47	.67
Millon (1987)	859	.47	.17	.56	.25	.22	.56	.62	.14	-.23	.79
Morey et al. (1985)	475	.48	-.05	.33	.31	.20	.59	.26	.39	.57	.60
Average		.57	.23	.56	.45	.41	.59	.52	.45	.25	.68
Dimension average		.45	.22	.42	.42	.35	.49	.42	.36	.13	.51
Total average[c]		.23	.03	.28	.36	.23	.35	.26	.27	-.02	.30

Note. n = total number of subjects sampled; PPD = paranoid; SZD = schizoid; SPD = schizotypal; HPD = histrionic; NPD = narcissistic; APD = antisocial; AVD = avoidant; DPD = dependent; CPD = compulsive; PAG = passive-aggressive.
[a]No cases of SZD or PAG found by Dubro et al. (1988) or Zanarini et al. (1987). [b]Dahl (1986) did not diagnose PAG in presence of other personality disorder. [c]Excludes Lyons et al. (1987) because sample overlaps with Hyler and Lyons (1988).

(Livesley and Jackson 1986), one was based on DSM-III-R (Morey 1988), another was based on a taxonomy similar but not equivalent to DSM-III-R (Millon 1987), three of the interview-based studies did not use semistructured interviews (Hyler and Lyons 1988; Kass et al. 1985; Morey 1988), and one of the studies used college seniors as interviewers (Widiger et al. 1987). Integrating these findings might be combining apples with oranges (Bangert-Drowns 1986). However, this diversity is also advantageous. Findings that are artifactual to a particular methodology will be evident by their lack of replication and will be neutralized by averaging across the studies (Cooper 1984; Rosenthal 1984). Averages of the correlations from the 6 interview categorical, the 3 interview dimensional, the 4 inventory dimensional, and all 12 studies that involved nonoverlapping data sets are also shown in Table 9-2 (averages were based on Fisher's r to z transformation values). Contrast analyses were performed on each respective set of correlations (Rosenthal 1984) and are shown in Table 9-3.

It is evident from Table 9-2 and 9-3 that research based on categorical data tends to provide lower correlations than research based on dimensional data. This finding was replicated across all 11 personality disorders. This is not a necessary or artifactual finding. It will not occur if the additional information provided by the dimensional rating is unreliable or invalid. Contrasts between the interview dimensional and interview categorical results for BPD were significant; however, only for PPD, AVD, and APD. There were more differences between the interview dimensional and inventory dimensional results. The pattern of correlations for the interview and inventory findings are also discrepant. The correlation between the 11 respective (r to z transformed) correlations for the category and inventory data was only .39 (Spearman rank-order correlation was only .19), whereas the correlation of the averaged correlations for the interview categorical and interview dimensional data was .80.

Previous research has indicated that self-report inventories tend to provide higher estimates of prevalence (Widiger and Frances 1987). The above findings suggest that they might also provide higher correlations among the personality disorders and perhaps even a different pattern of results. For example, the interview categorical data identified little to no correlation between BPD and PAG ($r = .09$) whereas the highest correlation for the inventory data was with PAG ($r = .68$). The Minnesota Multiphasic Personality Inventory (MMPI) personality disorder scales (Morey et al. 1985) and the Personality Diagnostic Questionnaire (Lyons et al. 1987) obtained substantial correlations with CPD ($r = .57$ and .47, respectively) that were not evident with any of the interview data. These differences are due to

Table 9-3. Contrast analyses on correlations with other personality disorders

Contrast	PPD	SZD	SPD	HPD	NPD	APD	AVD	DPD	CPD	PAG
D vs. C	8.65*	4.14*	5.96*	1.69	3.77*	6.13*	6.41*	2.88**	4.36*	8.73*
I-D vs. C	3.70*	1.45	1.17	.73	1.48	2.11**	2.58**	.32	.95	1.93
S-D vs. I-D	7.69*	4.27*	8.29*	1.49	3.63*	6.54*	6.04*	4.54*	5.85*	12.92*

Note. D = dimensional studies (interview and inventory); C = categorical studies; I-D = interview dimensional studies; S-D = self-report inventory dimensional studies; PPD = paranoid; SZD = schizoid; SPD = schizotypal; HPD = histrionic; NPD = narcissistic; APD = antisocial; AVD = avoidant; DPD = dependent; CPD = compulsive; PAG = passive-aggressive personality disorder. *P < .001. **P < .05.

the loss of reliable and valid information in a categorical analysis, with a resulting loss of power in statistical analyses. PPD, rated as absence in Pfohl et al. (1986), could still be given scores of 1–3 in Kass et al. (1985) and 0–13 in Widiger et al. (1987). However, the differences might also reflect the influence of state factors on the self-report inventory data (Reich 1987; Widiger and Frances 1987). Patients might have more difficulty distinguishing between their past and current Axis I clinical syndromes and their long-standing personality traits. This would not explain the uniformly high correlations obtained by Livesley and Jackson's (1986) subjects, because none had any substantial Axis I pathology, but the frequency of prototypic acts that were collected in this study might be providing inflated correlations.

Much of the variability in findings is due to idiosyncratic features of individual studies. Dubro et al. (1988) obtained a negative correlation with SPD (−.11) because they found only one case of SPD, and Frances et al. (1984) obtained a negative correlation with APD (−.12) because they found only two cases. Disorders that occur infrequently will tend to be negatively correlated with frequent disorders, particularly with a categorical analysis.

Averaging across the studies is helpful in neutralizing the idiosyncracies and perhaps providing a better estimate of the true pattern of correlations. The averaged correlations for BPD indicated that it covaried most highly with HPD, APD, and PAG, followed by SPD, DPD, AVD, NPD, and PPD. One might have expected a more substantial correlation with SPD, given that much of the comorbidity research for BPD has focused on this association (McGlashan 1987; Siever and Klar 1986). However, as we indicated earlier, even in studies where there is substantial co-occurrence there is often little significant covariation. BPD and SPD often co-occur perhaps because they are prevalent personality disorders at similar levels of severe pathology, but they do not correlate substantially because they involve different dimensions of pathology (Spitzer et al. 1979; Widiger et al. 1987). BPD might represent a characterologic variant along an affective/impulsivity spectrum of pathology and SPD a characterologic variant along a schizophrenic spectrum (Widiger et al. 1988).

The correlations with HPD and APD are consistent with theoretical expectations, as both are within the dramatic/emotional cluster of the DSM-III-R and are characterized by high levels of extraversion. The substantial correlation with PAG is not surprising because a substantial degree of hostile resistance and negativism will often be seen in borderline patients. However, it should also be noted that

BPD correlated with all of the personality disorders except the two with the lowest prevalence (SZD and CPD). The average correlation between the prevalence of the other personality disorders and their correlations with BPD across the six categorical studies was .72, with one as high as .95 (Zanarini et al. 1987). In other words, half of the variance in the correlation with BPD could be explained by the prevalence of the other disorder, perhaps again suggesting that BPD is a nonspecific diagnosis indicating a level of pathology or general neuroticism (Fyer et al. 1988).

Schizotypal Personality Disorder

Table 9-4 shows the covariations for SPD. Perhaps the most striking finding is the inconsistency of the results across the four categorical studies. The highest covariation in Pfohl et al. (1986) was with AVD (with no correlation with PPD, SZD, or HPD), whereas the highest covariations in Morey (1988) were with SZD and PPD. The highest covariation in Zanarini et al. (1987) was with HPD, whereas the only substantial correlation in Dahl (1986) was a negative correlation with HPD. This inconsistency may reflect the low power of categorical analyses and the low prevalence of BPD and SZD cases in Dahl (1986), Pfohl et al. (1986), and Zanarini et al. (1987). Results from the other studies are consistent in finding the highest covariation with PPD and secondarily with AVD, SZD, and BPD. These results reflect their sharing features of introversion (McCrae and Costa 1987; Widiger and Kelso 1983) and features of the odd-eccentric cluster of DSM-III-R.

The one exception to this finding was by Widiger et al. (1987). They reported a negative correlation with SZD due to their coding of any person who displayed schizotypal symptoms as negative for the DSM-III schizoid item of no eccentricities of speech, behavior, or thought characteristic of SPD. When this item was deleted the correlation fell from −.28 to .03. The SZD item was deleted in DSM-III-R (Widiger et al. 1988).

Avoidant Personality Disorder

Table 9-5 shows correlations for AVD. AVD was a new addition to DSM-III (Frances 1980; Millon 1981) and its inclusion generated considerable criticism, including the concern that it would be indistinguishable from SZD (Gunderson 1983; Livesley et al. 1985). However, in 6 of 10 studies, the highest correlation was with DPD, and in only 1 of 10 studies was its highest correlation with SZD (Hyler and Lyons 1988). It did correlate moderately with SZD in most of

Table 9-4. Covariation of schizotypal with other personality disorders

Study	n		Other personality disorders									
	Tot	Pd	PPD	SZD	HPD	NPD	APD	BPD	AVD	DPD	CPD	PAG
Pfohl et al. (1986)	131	12	-.03	-.03	.08	.07	.07	.21	.47	-.12	.16	.33
Zanarini et al. (1987)	43	15	.19		.31	.07	-.17	.29	.28	.16	.04	.03
Dahl (1986)	103	41	.12	.19	-.35	-.02	-.02	.08	-.04	-.16	-.08	
Morey (1988)	291	27	.31	.34	-.02	.09	-.03	.00	.23	.06	.04	.02
Hyler and Lyons (1988)	358	6	.33	.43	.08	.15	.09	.33	.25	.22	-.04	.13
Kass et al. (1985)	609	24	.42	.34	-.03	.03	.04	.19	.22	.01	.03	.02
Widiger et al. (1987)	84	53	.44	-.28	.06	.19	.15	.08	.30	.07	.31	.13
Livesley et al. (1986)	115		.63	.37	.38	.48	.46	.62	.52	.51	.10	.57
Morey et al. (1985)	475		.73	.36	-.11	-.08	.46	.38	.36	.40	.28	.63
Millon (1987)	769		.49	.46	-.19	.18	.28	.59	.70	.33	.04	.47
Average			.39	.25	.02	.12	.14	.30	.35	.16	.09	.24

Note. Tot = total number of subjects; Pd = number with schizotypal personality disorder; PPD = paranoid; SZD = schizoid; HPD = histrionic; NPD = narcissistic; APD = antisocial; AVD = avoidant; DPD = dependent; CPD = compulsive; PAG = passive-aggressive; BPD = borderline.

Table 9-5 Covariation of avoidant with other personality disorders

Study	n Tot	Pd	PPD	SZD	SPD	HPD	NPD	APD	BPD	DPD	CPD	PAG
									Other personality disorders			
Pfohl et al. (1986)	131	15	-.03	-.03	.47	.03	.05	.05	.15	.08	.13	.20
Zanarini et al. (1987)	43	15	.34		.28	.11	-.19	-.40	.39	.16	.19	-.10
Dahl (1986)	103	17	-.04	.26	-.04	-.33	-.08	-.26	-.29	.32	-.04	
Morey (1988)	291	79	.25	.21	.23	.05	.10	-.06	.14	.27	.19	.05
Hyler and Lyons (1988)	358	23	.17	.33	.25	.00	.03	.02	.19	.29	.18	.26
Kass et al. (1985)	609	30	.15	.17	.22	-.03	.03	.02	.19	.43	.08	.25
Widiger et al. (1987)	84	28	.08	-.25	.30	.20	-.18	.14	.40	.62	.06	.32
Livesley et al. (1986)	115		.68	.59	.52	.21	.39	.41	.63	.73	.14	.70
Morey et al. (1985)	475		.22	.42	.36	-.33	-.29	.21	.41	.57	.35	.31
Millon (1987)	769		.36	.46	.70	-.35	.03	.16	.54	.44	.03	.43
Average			.24	.25	.35	-.05	-.01	.03	.29	.42	.13	.29

Note. Tot = total number of subjects; Pd = number with avoidance personality disorder; PPD = paranoid; SZD = schizotypal; HPD = histrionic; NPD = narcissistic; AVD = avoidant; DPD = dependent; CPD = compulsive; PAG = passive-aggressive; BPD = borderline.

the studies, but not as consistently or as highly as with SPD, PAG, BPD, and DPD.

The correlation of AVD and DPD might not have been anticipated because they are seemingly quite different personality disorders. AVD involves social withdrawal and the avoidance of relations, whereas DPD involves an overinvolvement and a clinging to relationships. However, AVD and DPD both involve a strong desire for interpersonal relationships, low self-confidence, and interpersonal insecurity. A lonely person who intensely desires involvements is likely to be very fearful of losing a relationship (i.e., dependent) once it has been established (Trull et al. 1987). The criteria sets for AVD and DPD were substantially revised in DSM-III-R. DSM-III-R criteria for AVD include additional features of the psychoanalytic concepts of the inhibited phobic character, such as an exaggeration of risks in everyday life and an inordinate fear of being embarrassed (Widiger et al. 1987). The DPD revision includes nine rather than just three items, including indicators of submissiveness and fears of separation. However, the new AVD and DPD items might still be common in patients with either disorder. Morey (1988), using an early draft of the DSM-III-R criteria, still found the highest correlation of AVD to be with DPD.

AVD and DPD could be distinguished easily by requiring all AVD patients to exhibit social withdrawal (it is now an optional criterion) and by including in the criteria for DPD indicators of the tendency to quickly form new relationships when a previous relationship ends. AVD and DPD are most similar when the person is interpersonally involved. It is in between relationships that they are readily distinguished. AVD persons tend to be shy, hesitant, and slow to initiate relationships, whereas DPD persons tend to be hasty and unselective.

Compulsive Personality Disorder

Table 9-6 presents the correlations for CPD. The most interesting finding is the absence of any substantial correlation in almost all of the studies. The only exception was by Morey et al. (1985) with the MMPI scales ($r = .58$ with BPD and $r = .53$ with PAG) which might be providing an idiosyncratic measure of CPD (perhaps emphasizing the ruminative and indecisiveness features of CPD).

CPD appears to be a high functioning personality disorder (Kernberg 1984) that includes achievement-oriented traits that are not often seen in other personality disordered patients, such as perfectionism and excessive devotion to work and productivity (i.e., conscientiousness in the five-factor model of personality; McCrae and Costa 1987). In their factor analysis of their correlations among the

Table 9-6. Covariation of compulsive with other personality disorders

Study	n		Other personality disorders									
	Tot	Pd	PPD	SZD	SPD	HPD	NPD	APD	BPD	AVD	DPD	PAG
Pfohl et al. (1986)	131	7	-.02	-.02	.16	.11	.13	-.05	.04	.13	.00	.20
Zanarini et al. (1987)	43	5	.09	.04	.04	-.15	-.16	-.20	-.16	.19	.08	.01
Dahl (1986)	103	1	.00	-.02	-.08	-.07	-.02	-.07	-.08	-.04	-.02	
Morey (1988)	291	23	.00	.10	.04	-.06	.06	-.08	-.15	.19	-.22	.12
Hyler and Lyons (1988)	358	40	.11	.06	-.04	-.02	.11	-.03	-.08	.18	.03	.24
Kass et al. (1985)	609	12	.04	.05	.03	-.04	.15	-.10	-.05	.08	.05	.14
Widiger et al. (1987)	84	2	.19	.19	.31	.23	.10	.18	-.01	.06	-.04	.14
Livesley et al. (1986)	115		.11	-.06	.10	.17	.06	-.11	.11	.14	.14	-.11
Morey et al. (1985)	475		.32	.00	.28	.30	.16	.23	.58	.35	.44	.53
Millon (1987)	769		.23	.12	.04	.09	.05	.03	-.05	.03	.25	.01
Average			.11	.05	.09	.05	.06	-.02	.02	.13	.08	.15

Note. Tot = total number of subjects; Pd = number with compulsive personality disorder; PPD = paranoid; SZD = schizoid; SPD = schizotypal; HPD = histrionic; NPD = narcissistic; APD = antisocial; AVD = avoidant; DPD = dependent; PAG = passive-aggressive; BPD = borderline.

personality disorders, Hyler and Lyons (1988) and Kass et al. (1985) found that CPD defined its own fourth factor.

The DSM-III-R revision of CPD (called "obsessive-compulsive personality disorder" in DSM-III-R) includes additional features of the original psychoanalytic constructs of parsimony and orderliness (Frances and Widiger 1987; Widiger et al. 1988), but it does not appear to be closer to any of the other personality disorders. The new item of overconscientiousness, scrupulousness, and inflexibility might further differentiate CPD from other personality disorders. CPD is perhaps closest to the maladaptive personality style referred to as Type A (Garamoni and Schwartz 1986), which is most often seen in highly competitive and achievement-oriented persons (although the Type A pattern might involve facets of antagonism rather than an excessive conscientiousness; Dembroski and Costa 1987). Neither CPD nor Type A are commonly seen in the psychiatric inpatient and community mental health outpatient clinics that are most often sampled in psychodiagnostic research. The covariation and comorbidity of CPD with some of the other personality disorders (e.g., NPD, AVD, and PAG) might be higher in samples obtained from private practice or other settings that involve a higher functioning population (Frances and Widiger 1987; Siever and Klar 1986).

Passive-Aggressive Personality Disorder

Table 9-7 provides the correlations for PAG. The findings from Dahl (1986) were not included because he did not diagnose PAG in the presence of any other personality disorder, artifactually resulting in no comorbidity. The results are comparable to BPD in that PAG correlated with most if not all of the other personality disorders. But unlike BPD, the pattern of correlations is neither consistent across nor even within methodologies. If one considers the two highest correlations, PAG correlated with BPD and SPD (Pfohl et al. (1986), DPD and PPD (Zanarini et al. 1987), APD and NPD, AVD and DPD (Kass et al. 1985), APD and AVD (Widiger et al. 1987), PPD and AVD (Livesley and Jackson 1986), PPD and SPD (Morey et al. 1985), BPD and PPD or SPD (Millon 1987), and DPD and NPD or APD (Hyler and Lyons 1988).

PAG was almost not included in DSM-III because it was considered by some to be a nonspecific situational reaction to being a powerless subordinate rather than a distinct personality disorder (Frances and Widiger 1987; Gunderson 1983). PAG might also be overdiagnosed in inpatient clinical settings as a result of a tendency of patients to resort to passive resistance to treatment demands and inpatient restrictions (Widiger and Frances 1985). The DSM-III exclusion criterion

Table 9-7. Covariation of passive-aggressive with other personality disorders[a]

Study	n Tot	n Pd	PPD	SZD	SPD	HPD	NPD	APD	BPD	AVD	DPD	CPD
Pfohl et al. (1986)	131	18	.22	-.03	.33	.26	.04	.27	.43	.20	.04	.20
Zanarini et al. (1987)	43	8	.20		.03	.10	-.05	.16	-.10	-.10	.21	.01
Morey (1988)	291	36	.08	.07	.02	.11	.25	.29	.02	.05	.07	.12
Hyler and Lyons (1988)	358	21	.25	.17	.13	.15	.28	.28	.16	.26	.38	.24
Kass et al. (1985)	609	12	.03	.01	.02	.10	.17	.04	.16	.25	.28	.14
Widiger et al. (1987)	84	44	.08	.10	.13	.16	.21	.31	.22	.32	.27	.14
Livesley et al. (1986)	115		.75	.59	.57	.33	.58	.68	.69	.70	.63	-.11
Morey et al. (1985)	475		.65	.09	.63	.27	.30	.54	.59	.31	.52	.53
Millon (1987)	769		.47	.14	.47	.09	.31	.38	.70	.43	.29	.01
Average			.33	.15	.28	.18	.24	.34	.35	.29	.31	.15

Note. Tot = total number of subjects; Pd = number with passive-aggressive personality disorder; PPD = paranoid; SZD = schizoid; SPD = schizotypal; HPD = histrionic; NPD = narcissistic; APD = antisocial; AVD = avoidant; DPD = dependent; CPD = compulsive; BPD = borderline.

that PAG be diagnosed only when no other personality disorder diagnosis applied, was to ensure that it be used only when it appeared to refer to a distinct, unique personality style. However, this exclusion criterion has been ignored in almost of all of the psychodiagnostic studies and was not included in the DSM-III-R revision (Widiger et al. 1988).

The results presented in Table 9-7 might support the argument that PAG does not describe a particular personality style but instead refers to a nonspecific behavior pattern. A failure to be correlated with any personality disorder would support the argument that the disorder describes a unique personality style, but PAG appears to correlate with all of them in a nonspecific and inconsistent manner. It is possible though that the DSM-III-R formulation will result in more consistent findings, describing a personality style that is closer to Millon's (1981) concept of negativism and the five-factor concept of antagonism (McCrae and Costa 1987).

DIMENSIONAL MODEL

The degree of co-occurrence and covariation is consistent with the suggestion that a dimensional model would be more appropriate than the categorical in the classification of personality disorders (Cloninger 1987; Costa and McCrae 1986b; Frances 1982; Widiger and Frances 1985). We will discuss in this section the alternative dimensional models that have been proposed, the inconsistency in the multivariate studies that have attempted to identify the underlying dimensions, and our own meta-analytic factor analysis and multidimensional scaling that tend to support the five-factor model.

There are numerous dimensional models of personality and personality disorders to choose from (Costa and McCrae 1986a; Frances and Widiger 1986). Cloninger suggests that three basic stimuli-response neurologically based learning mechanisms of novelty seeking, harm avoidance, and reward dependence underlie the manifestation and variation among the personality disorders. Millon (1981, 1986) suggests that personality disorders reflect pathological deficits or imbalances in the nature (pleasure versus pain), source (self versus other), or instrumental behaviors (active versus passive) that persons use. Eysenck and Eysenck (1985) have proposed that three basic dimensions of neuroticism (instability and emotionality), psychoticism (impulsivity, aggression, tough mindedness, and egocentricity), and extraversion (sociability, activity, assertiveness, sensation seeking, and dominance) define the domain of psychopathology. Tellegen (1985) has more recently formulated three broad dimensions of positive emotionality, negative emotionality, and constraint. Kiesler (1986), Benjamin (1987), Wiggins (1982), and Widiger and Kelso (1983) have suggested that personality disorders are fundamentally disorders of interpersonal style. It is also conceivable that some of the personality disorders represent characterological variants along Axis I spectra of pathology that are now represented by the three clusters. BPD could be along an impulsivity/affectivity spectrum, SPD along a schizophrenic spectrum, and AVD along an anxiety spectrum (Siever et al. 1985; Widiger et al. 1988).

We have in the past recommended the interpersonal circumplex as a viable model, but research has suggested that the circumplex might be readily accounted for by the extraversion and agreeableness dimensions of the five-factor (or Big Five) model of personality (Costa and McCrae 1986b; McCrae and Costa 1987; Wiggins 1987) and the variance among the personality disorders does not appear to be readily explained by just two interpersonal factors (Widiger and Kelso 1983; Widiger et al. 1987; J.S. Wiggins and A.L. Pincus, 1988, unpublished observations). Personality disorders, at least as they are currently defined, include additional dimensions of pathology. The openness, conscientiousness, and neuroticism dimensions of the five-factor model might account for the additional variance (J.S. Wiggins and A.L. Pincus, 1988, unpublished observations). Neuroticism includes facets of trait anxiety, hostility, depression, self-consciousness, impulsivity, and vulnerability (Costa and McCrae 1985) on which all of the personality disorders would load, particularly BPD. It might represent a general measure of the degree of personality dysfunction. Openness would at first appear to lack a clear pathological variant, but pathological openness might be expressed in the schizotypal's loose ideation, fringe interests, and magical thinking, and in the histrionic's fluctuating affect (P.T. Costa and R.R. McCrae, 13 December 1988, personal communication). Lack of openness includes a narrow range of emotions, insensitivity to surroundings, preference for the familiar, and strict routines, dogmatism, and conformity, which are readily evident in the schizoid, compulsive, and/or avoidant. The conscientiousness dimension is useful in representing CPD. Disorders low in conscientiousness might include BPD, APD, and PAG.

Six studies have attempted to identify empirically the dimensions that define or underlie DSM-III personality disorders (Blashfield et al. 1985; Hyler and Lyons 1988; Kass et al. 1985; Millon 1987; Morey et al. 1985; Widiger et al. 1987). There is no obvious consistency in their findings (Morey 1986), perhaps because of the substantial variability in the methodologies that have been used. The studies varied in the number of factors/dimensions extracted (from 2 to 4), the statistical analyses (multidimensional scaling and factor analyses), the method of data collection (clinical interviews, self-report inventories, and analogue case histories), and theoretical models defining the disorders being assessed. We attempted to identify some consistency by correlating the factor and scaling loadings across the studies (the findings from Hyler and Lyons 1988 could not be considered because only the loadings greater than 50 were reported).

The third dimension obtained by Kass et al. (1985) appears to be the most consistently replicated across the other studies, correlating highly with the second dimension in Widiger et al. (1987; $r = .79$), the first dimension in Blashfield et al. (1985; $r = .67$), the first factor in Morey et al. (1985; $r = .84$), and the third factor in Millon (1987; $r = .77$). However, these researchers did not provide the same interpretations for the respective dimensions/factors. Kass et al. interpreted it as representing the dramatic/emotional cluster, with the highest loadings by NPD, BPD, HPD, and APD (disorders are presented here and will be presented below in the rank order of their factor or scaling loadings), and Morey et al. interpreted it as representing the anxious/fearful cluster, with the highest loadings by DPD, CPD, and BPD and the lowest by SZD, HPD, and PAG. Widiger et al. interpreted it as representing assertion/dominance, contrasting NPD, HPD, BPD, and PPD with SZD, PAG, AVD, and DPD, and Blashfield et al. interpreted it as representing interpersonal involvement, contrasting PPD and CPD with BPD, APD, and HPD. Millon interpreted it as representing sociability and self-confidence versus schizoid detachment and thought, with substantial negative loadings by HPD and NPD and positive loadings by SZD and AVD. Widiger et al. and Blashfield et al. interpreted their first dimensions similarly, with Widiger et al. describing it as social involvement and Blashfield et al. describing it as interpersonal involvement, yet these two dimensions obtained a low and negative correlation of $-.28$. Kass et al. and Morey et al. interpreted their third and second dimensions, respectively, as representing the dramatic/emotional cluster, but they obtained a very low (but at least positive) correlation of .28. The major difficulty in integrating and interpreting these factor analytic and multidimensional scaling solutions is that none of the studies provided an independent measure of the dimensions by which they were interpreting their results. The DSM-III personality disorders are heterogeneous in their definitions, and it is very difficult to reach a consensus as to how to interpret a rank ordering.

One solution to the problem of different methodologies is to aggregate the results, minimizing the effect of idiosyncratic and unreplicated findings. We averaged the correlations of the personality disorders across nine studies (Dahl 1986; Kass et al. 1985; Livesley and Jackson 1986; Millon 1987; Morey 1988; Morey et al. 1985; Pfohl et al. 1986; Widiger et al. 1987; Zanarini et al. 1987) using the formula for this meta-analysis presented by Rosenthal (1984). Table 9-8 presents these averaged correlations.

The averaged correlations were then submitted to both a multidimensional scaling (ALSCAL) and a factor analysis (principal components). Both forms of analyses were used because both have been used in previous studies. Table 9-9 shows the four dimensional and four-factor solutions. A four-factor solution to the factor analysis was optimal, using scree and 1.0 eigenvalue criteria. The one-, two-, three-, four-, and five-factor solutions obtained eigenvalues of 2.9, 2.6, 1.2, 1.0, and .8, respectively, and the cumulative proportions of variance accounted for were .27, .42, .53, .62, and .69, respectively. A three dimensional solution of the multidimensional scaling would have been optimal using the .10 stress value criterion. The two, three, and four dimensional solutions obtained stress values of .16, .07, and .05, respectively, and the cumulative proportions of variance accounted for were .83, .96, and .97, respectively. However, we are reporting the four dimensional multidimensional scaling solution to

Table 9-8. Correlation among personality disorders averaged across nine studies[a]

Disorder	PPD	SZD[b]	SPD	HPD	NPD	APD	BPD	AVD	DPD	CPD
SZD	.22									
SPD	.39	.23								
HPD	.08	−.19	.02							
NPD	.24	.03	.11	.35						
APD	.23	.12	.15	.24	.33					
BPD	.22	.05	.29	.39	.19	.37				
AVD	.24	.24	.36	−.05	−.01	.03	.30			
DPD	.10	.04	.15	.15	−.01	.07	.30	.42		
CPD	.11	.05	.10	.06	.06	−.02	.03	.13	.08	
PAG[c]	.34	.15	.25	.18	.24	.35	.38	.29	.30	.14

Note. PPD = paranoid; SZD = schizoid; SPD = schizotypal; HPD = histrionic; NPD = narcissistic; APD = antisocial; AVD = avoidant; DPD = dependent; CPD = compulsive; PAG = passive-aggressive; BPD = borderline. [a]Pfohl et al. (1986), Zanarini et al. (1987), Dahl (1986), Morey (1988), Kass et al. (1985), Widiger et al. (1987), Livesley and Jackson (1986), Morey et al. (1985), Millon (1987). [b]Excludes Zanarini et al. (1987) because no SZD cases were identified. [c]Excludes Dahl (1986) because PAG not diagnosed in presence of any other personality disorders.

allow a comparison of the factor analytic and multidimensional scaling solutions. The first three dimensions of the four dimensional multidimensional scaling were essentially identical to the three dimensions of the three dimensional solution.

The factor analytic and multidimensional scaling solutions are essentially identical for three of the dimensions. The first dimension of the multidimensional scaling correlated .98 with the second (unrotated) factor (factor loadings were converted with Fisher's r to z transformations), the second dimension correlated .98 with the third (unrotated) factor, and the third dimension correlated .87 with the fourth (unrotated) factor. The first (unrotated) factor correlated only $-.38$ with the fourth multidimensional scaling dimension. The unrotated factor solution is being presented because the rotated solution is somewhat less similar to the multidimensional scaling and is no more interpretable. The respective correlations for a varimax rotated solution are $-.91$, $-.86$, $-.81$, and $-.25$, respectively (the order of the factors changed, with the first factor becoming the third factor).

The replication failures are perhaps understandable. The fourth dimension in the multidimensional scaling accounted for only 1% of additional variance over the three dimensional solution and might be uninterpretable. In addition, the first factor of a principal components factor analysis is often a general factor, with heavy loadings by all of the variables. This is evident in Table 9-9. In addition, the two poles

Table 9-9. Multidimensional scaling and factor analytic solutions for averaged correlations

Disorder	Multidimensional scaling				Factor analysis (unrotated)			
	1	2	3	4	1	2	3	4
PPD	.4	1.1	$-.1$	-1.0	.59	.13	.39	.11
SZD	2.0	1.4	$-.0$	.8	.30	.48	.47	$-.15$
SPD	1.2	.3	$-.3$	-1.3	.59	.33	.19	.01
HPD	-2.2	$-.8$	.3	.0	.38	$-.67$	$-.27$	.13
NPD	-1.7	1.2	.4	$-.1$	.43	$-.51$	.33	.17
APD	-1.2	1.0	$-.8$	.8	.53	$-.40$	.27	$-.25$
BPD	$-.8$	$-.7$	$-.8$	$-.1$	.68	$-.21$	$-.27$	$-.21$
AVD	1.7	$-.9$	$-.4$	.0	.55	.53	$-.29$	$-.05$
DPD	.5	-2.0	$-.3$	.5	.47	.21	$-.64$	$-.09$
CPD	.4	$-.4$	2.6	.2	.21	.14	$-.06$	.90
PAG	$-.2$	$-.2$	$-.8$	.1	.71	$-.01$	$-.01$	.01

Note. PPD = paranoid; SZD = schizoid; SPD = schizotypal; HPD = histrionic; NPD = narcissistic; APD = antisocial; AVD = avoidant; DPD = dependent; CPD = compulsive; PAG = passive-aggressive; BPD = borderline.

of this solution are PAG and BPD versus CPD. PAG was the one personality disorder with moderately high and nonspecific correlations with all of the personality disorders, and CPD was the one personality disorder with no correlations with hardly any personality disorder. PAG loaded only on this factor. This factor might then be a nonspecific factor and/or a general factor of neuroticism (Costa and McCrae 1986b).

The third dimension of the multidimensional scaling solution and the fourth factor of the factor analysis, respectively, are clearly CPD factors, replicating the findings of Hyler and Lyons (1988) and Kass et al. (1985). The factor appears to contrast CPD with other personality disorders, perhaps as a result of the failure of CPD to obtain substantial correlations with any other personality disorder (i.e., a single factor was necessary to account for its variance). One might then consider this factor to be artifactual. However, it could also be interpreted as representing the conscientiousness dimension from the five-factor model (McCrae and Costa 1987). It contrasts the one personality disorder that is clearly high on conscientiousness with the three that are low (i.e., APD, BPD, and PAG).

Figure 9-1 provides a plot of the multidimensional scaling loadings for the remaining two dimensions that were replicated across the multidimensional scaling and factor analytic solutions and are some-

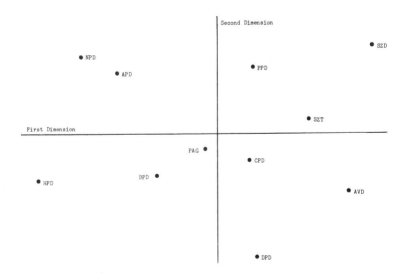

Figure 9-1. Multidimensional scaling loadings for averaged correlations.

what more difficult to interpret (i.e., the first and second dimensions of the multidimensional scaling and the second and third factors of the unrotated factor analysis which correlated .98 with the multidimensional scaling dimensions, respectively). The first dimension could be contrasting the dramatic/emotional cluster (HPD, NPD, APD, and BPD) with the odd-eccentric cluster (SZD, SPD, and PPD). The anxious/fearful cluster is not represented by any particular dimension because of the nonspecific correlations of PAG and the low correlations of CPD. The latter two diagnoses are toward the center of the axes. However, one can clearly demarcate the three clusters in the figure without any overlap. In this respect, the results support Hyler and Lyons (1988) and Kass et al. (1985) and DSM-III-R clustering.

However, one difficulty with the interpretation of the first dimension as contrasting dramatic-emotional with odd-eccentric is the placement of AVD. It is difficult to interpret this pole as being the odd-eccentric cluster with AVD being the second highest personality disorder on this dimension. An alternative interpretation is to rotate the axes 45° (the placement of the axes is arbitrary), such that the horizontal axis cuts through SZD and the vertical through APD-NPD. The new horizontal axis is now readily interpreted as contrasting extraverted personality disorders (HPD, BPD, NPD, DPD, and APD) with introverted (SZD, SPD, and PPD). AVD is halfway between SZD and HPD-DPD because it represents a mixture of social isolation and dependency. The new vertical axis could represent dominance (NPD, APD, HPD, and PPD) versus submission (AVD, DPD, and SZD). In this respect, the results support Widiger et al. (1987).

However, these interpretations are again quite subjective. The solution obtained from the aggregated correlations might be a reliable solution, but any interpretation of the factors will still be debatable until independent measures of the constructs are obtained and correlated to the factor and/or multidimensional solution. We recommend that future studies include independent measures of the constructs that will likely be used to interpret the findings. Unfortunately, there are no adequate measures of the clinical spectra (most scales confine themselves to a limited range along the spectra) nor for the self-other, pleasure-pain, and active-passive dimensions of Millon (1981, 1986). However, there are self-report inventories to assess the five-factor model (Costa and McCrae 1985), the interpersonal circumplex (Wiggins 1982; J.S. Wiggins and A.L. Pincus, 1988, unpublished observations) and the dimensions proposed by Benjamin (1987), Cloninger (1987), Eysenck and Eysenck (1985), and Tellegen (1985).

CONCLUSION

The comorbidity, co-occurrence, and covariation among personality disorders is extensive, particularly for BPD. An implication of this review for clinical practice is that clinicians should not rest with just one personality disorder diagnosis. Chart review research has obtained fewer personality disorder diagnoses than are obtained when semi-structured interviews are used (Pfohl et al. 1986). Practicing clinicians rarely give more than two and usually just one personality disorder diagnosis. However, semistructured interviews have obtained an average of 3.75 (Widiger et al. 1986a) and 4.6 (Skodol et al. 1988) personality disorder diagnoses per patient. Either practicing clinicians are not providing a comprehensive description of their patients' personality disorder pathology or the DSM-III-R criteria sets are overly inclusive and redundant.

The direction and pattern of co-occurrence, however, is consistent with clinical and theoretical expectations. Interpreting this pattern though is complicated by a variety of different substantive and methodological explanations for comorbidity that have not been addressed or distinguished in the research. In addition, no study has yet demonstrated that the DSM-III-R diagnoses identify distinct personality types, and the co-occurrence data suggest that this is unlikely to occur, at least as the disorders are currently defined.

A dimensional model of classification would be more comprehensive, exact, and consistent with the research, and might even be simpler to use than the categorical. The categorical system results in many atypical and literally borderline cases, and multiple diagnoses can become so extensive as to be more confusing than informative. However, research concerned with the identification of the dimensions that would be optimal in defining and diagnosing personality disorder has not provided consistent results due to the variation in methodology across studies. There is a need to include independent measures of the various constructs that have been used to interpret the factor analytic and multidimensional scaling solutions. These measures can be correlated empirically to the solutions to provide a more objective interpretation of the results.

REFERENCES

American Psychiatric Association: Diagnostic and Statistical Manual of Mental Disorders, 3rd Edition. Washington, DC, American Psychiatric Association, 1980

American Psychiatric Association: Diagnostic and Statistical Manual of Mental Disorders, 3rd Edition, Revised. Washington, DC, American Psychiatric Association, 1987

Bangert-Drowns R: Review of developments in meta-analytic method. Psychol Bull 99:388–399, 1986

Benjamin LS: Use of the SASB dimensional model to develop treatment plans for personality disorders, I: narcissism. J Pers Disord 1:43–70, 1987

Blashfield R, Sprock J, Pinkston K, et al: Exemplar prototypes of personality disorder diagnosis. Compr Psychiatry 26:11–21, 1985

Boyd J, Burke J, Gruenberg E, et al: Exclusion criteria of DSM-III: a study of co-occurrences of hierarchy-free syndromes. Arch Gen Psychiatry 41:983–989, 1984

Cloninger CR: A systematic method for clinical description and classification of personality traits. Arch Gen Psychiatry 44:573–588, 1987

Cooper HM: The Integrative Research Review. Beverly Hills, CA, Sage, 1984

Costa PT, McCrae RR: The NEO Personality Inventory Manual. Odessa, FL, Psychological Assessment Resources, 1985

Costa PT, McCrae RR: Major contributions to the psychology of personality, in Hans Eysenck: Consensus and Controversy. Edited by Modgil S, Modgil C. London, The Falmer Press, 1986a, pp 63–72

Costa PT, McCrae RR: Personality stability and its implications for clinical psychology. Clin Psychol Rev 6:407–423, 1986b

Dahl A: Some aspects of the DSM-III personality disorders illustrated by a consecutive sample of hospitalized patients. Acta Psychiatr Scand 73:62–66, 1986

Dembroski TM, Costa PT: Coronary prone behavior: components of the Type A pattern and hostility. J Pers 55:211–235, 1987

Dubro AF, Wetzler S, Kahn MW: A comparison of three self-report questionnaires for the diagnosis of DSM-III personality disorders. J Pers Disord 2:256–266, 1988

Eysenck H, Eysenck M: Personality and Individual Differences: A Natural Science Approach. New York, Plenum, 1985

Frances A: The DSM-III personality disorders section: a commentary. Am J Psychiatry 137:1050–1054, 1980

Frances A: Categorical and dimensional systems of personality diagnosis: a comparison. Compr Psychiatry 23:516–527, 1982

Frances AJ, Widiger T: The classification of personality disorders: an overview of problems and solutions, in Psychiatry Update: American Psychiatric Association Annual Review, Vol 5. Edited by Frances AJ, Hales RE. Washington, DC, American Psychiatric Press, 1986, pp 240–257

Frances A, Widiger T: A critical review of four DSM-III personality disorders: borderline, avoidant, dependent, and passive-aggressive, in Diagnosis and Classification in Psychiatry: A Critical Appraisal of DSM-III. Edited by Tischler GL. New York, Cambridge University Press, 1987

Frances A, Clarkin J, Gilmore M, et al: Reliability of criteria for borderline personality disorder: a comparison of DSM-III and the diagnostic interview for borderline patients. Am J Psychiatry 141:1080–1084, 1984

Frances A, Widiger T, Fyer MR: The influence of classification methods on comorbidity, in Comorbidity of Mood and Anxiety Disorders. Edited by Maser J, Cloninger CR. Washington, DC, American Psychiatric Press, 1990, pp 41–59

Fyer M, Frances A, Sullivan T, et al: Comorbidity of borderline personality disorder. Arch Gen Psychiatry 45:348–352, 1988

Garamoni G, Schwartz R: Type A behavior pattern and compulsive personality: toward a psychodynamic-behavioral integration. Clin Psychol Rev 6:311–336, 1986

Gunderson J: DSM-III diagnosis of personality disorders, in Current Perspectives on Personality Disorders. Edited by Frosch J. Washington, DC, American Psychiatric Press, 1983, pp 20–39

Gunderson J, Zanarini M: Current overview of the borderline diagnosis. J Clin Psychiatry 48 (Suppl):5–11, 1987

Hyler S, Lyons M: Factor analysis of the DSM-III personality disorder clusters: a replication. Compr Psychiatry 29:304–308, 1988

Kass F, Skodol A, Charles E, et al: Scaled ratings of DSM-III personality disorders. Am J Psychiatry 142:627–630, 1985

Kernberg O: Severe Personality Disorders. New Haven, CT, Yale University Press, 1984

Kiesler D: The 1982 interpersonal circle: an analysis of DSM-III personality disorders. In Contemporary Directions in Psychopathology: Toward the DSM-IV. Edited by Millon T, Klerman G. New York, Guilford, 1986, pp 571–597

Livesley WJ, Jackson D: The internal consistency and factorial structure of behaviors judged to be associated with DSM-III personality disorders. Am J Psychiatry 143:1473–1474, 1986

Livesley WJ, West M, Tanney A: Historical comment on DSM-III schizoid and avoidant personality disorders. Am J Psychiatry 142:1344–1347, 1985

Lyons M, Hyler S, Rieder R, et al: The Factor Structure of Self-Reported DSM-III Personality Disorder Symptoms. Paper presented at the annual meeting of the American Psychological Association, New York, 28 August 1987

McCrae RR, Costa PT: Validation of the five-factor model of personality across instruments and observers. J Pers Soc Psychol 52:81–90, 1987

McGlashan T: Testing DSM-III symptom criteria for schizotypal and borderline personality disorders. Arch Gen Psychiatry 44:143–148, 1987

Millon T: Disorders of Personality: DSM-III. Axis II. New York, John Wiley, 1981

Millon T: A theoretical derivation of pathological personalities, in Contemporary Directions in Psychopathology. Edited by Millon T, Klerman G. New York, Guilford, 1986, pp 639–669

Millon T: Manual for the MCMI-III. Minneapolis, MN, National Computer Systems, 1987

Morey L: A comparison of three personality disorder assessment approaches. J Psychopathol Behav Assess 8:25–30, 1986

Morey L: Personality disorders under DSM-III and DSM-III-R: an examination of convergence, coverage, and internal consistency. Am J Psychiatry 145:573–577, 1988

Morey L, Waugh M, Blashfield R: MMPI scales for DSM-III personality disorders: their derivation and correlates. J Pers Assess 49:245–251, 1985

Pfohl B, Coryell W, Zimmerman M, et al: DSM-III personality disorders: diagnostic overlap and internal consistency of individual DSM-III criteria. Compr Psychiatry 27:21–34, 1986

Pope H, Jonas J, Hudson J, et al: The validity of DSM-III borderline personality disorder. Arch Gen Psychiatry 40:23–30, 1983

Reich J: Instruments measuring DSM-III and DSM-III-R personality disorders. J Pers Disord 1:220–240, 1987

Rosenthal R: Meta-Analytic Procedures for Social Research. Beverly Hills, CA, Sage, 1984

Siever LJ, Klar H: A review of DSM-III criteria for the personality disorders, in Psychiatry Update: American Psychiatric Association Annual Review,

Vol 5. Edited by Frances AJ, Hales RE. Washington, DC, American Psychiatric Press, 1986, pp 279–314

Siever LJ, Klar H, Coccaro E: Psychobiologic substrates of personality, in Biologic Response Styles: Clinical Implications. Edited by Klar H, Siever LJ. Washington, DC, American Psychiatric Press, 1985, pp 37–66

Skodol AE, Rosnick L, Kellman D, et al: Validating structured DSM-III-R personality disorder assessments with longitudinal data. Am J Psychiatry 145:1297–1299, 1988

Spitzer R, Endicott J, Gibbon M: Crossing the border into borderline personality and borderline schizophrenia: the development of criteria. Arch Gen Psychiatry 36:17–24, 1979

Tellegen A: Structures of mood and personality and their relevance to assessing anxiety, with an emphasis on self-report, in Anxiety and the Anxiety Disorders. Edited by Tuma AH, Maser JD. Hillsdale, NJ, Lawrence Erlbaum, 1985, pp 681–706

Torgersen S: Genetic and nosological aspects of schizotypal and borderline personality disorders. Arch Gen Psychiatry 41:546–554, 1984

Trull T, Widiger T, Frances A: Covariation of criteria sets for avoidant, schizoid, and dependent personality disorders. Am J Psychiatry 144:767–771, 1987

Widiger T, Frances A: The DSM-III personality disorders: perspectives from psychology. Arch Gen Psychiatry 42:615–623, 1985

Widiger T, Frances A: Interviews and inventories for the measurement of personality disorders. Clin Psychol Rev 7:49–75, 1987

Widiger T, Kelso K: Psychodiagnosis of Axis II. Clin Psychol Rev 3:491–510, 1983

Widiger T, Frances A, Warner L, et al: Diagnostic criteria for the borderline and schizotypal personality disorders. J Abnorm Psychol 95:43–51, 1986a

Widiger T, Sanderson C, Warner L: The MMPI, prototypal typology, and borderline personality disorder. J Pers Assess 50:540–553, 1986b

Widiger T, Trull T, Hurt S, et al: A multidimensional scaling of the DSM-III personality disorders. Arch Gen Psychiatry 44:557–563, 1987

Widiger T, Frances A, Spitzer R, et al: The DSM-III-R personality disorders: an overview. Am J Psychiatry 145:786–795, 1988

Wiggins JS: Circumplex models of interpersonal behavior in clinical psychology, in Handbook of Research Methods in Clinical Psychology. Edited by Kendall P, Butcher J. New York, John Wiley, 1982, pp 183–221

Wiggins JS: How Interpersonal Are the MMPI Personality Disorder Scales? Paper presented at the annual meeting of the American Psychological Association, New York, 1 September 1987

Zanarini M, Frankenburg F, Chauncey D, et al: The diagnostic interview for personality disorders: interrater and test-retest reliability. Compr Psychiatry 28:467–480, 1987

Index